BUT ONCE A YEAR

A Christmas Comedy in Three Acts

by

FALKLAND L. CARY

Revised Edition

LONDON

SAMUEL FRENCH LIMITED

To
RICHARD EASTHAM
and
ANTHONY ALLISON
in gratitude

But Once A Year was first presented at The Empire Theatre, Peterborough, by Mr Harry Hanson's Court Players, with the following cast:

Mary Meldon	GRACE POOLE
Ann Meldon (*her young daughter*)	BUNTY LEATON
Olivia Meldon (*her elder daughter*)	JANE HILARY
Ned Meldon (*their uncle*)	IVAN BUTLER
Topsey Richards (*their aunt*)	MOLLY REDMOND
Enid Martley	VIVIEN HAGUE
Tony Martley (*her son*)	STANLEY BRIDGER
George Linsitt	JOHN TOWNSEND
Alice	JOAN CONGDON
Mr Nicholas	REGINALD BARRATT

The Play Designed and Produced by RICHARD EASTHAM

The Amateur Première of *But Once a Year* was given by the Epiphany Players at St Peter's Hall, Bournemouth, with the following cast:

Mary Meldon	IVY DOWSE
Ann Meldon	RITA DAVIES
Alice	MARGARET DAVIS
Topsey Richards	MURIEL CLARK
Tony Martley	DOUGLAS DALTON
Enid Martley	MADGE JAMES
Olivia Meldon	SHEILA PENNEY
Ned Meldon	NORMAN DALLEN
Mr Nicholas	LESLIE SMITH
George Linsitt	PHILIP WARD

The Play Produced by ANTHONY ALLISON

To face page 1, "But Once a Year".

ACT I

Scene.—*The lounge at "Garlands". The evening of Christmas Eve.*

There are doors up L. *and* R. *In the back wall* L. *are french windows and* R. *an archway to the hall, where the stairs are visible. The wall* L. *of the hall has a window. In the wall* L. *is a fireplace. It is a comfortable and well-used room, nicely and tastefully furnished. The furniture consists of a settee, writing table, two armchairs, radiogram, two small tables, coffee table, chair, standard lamp and a Christmas tree. A clock and a table can be seen in the hall. The room is decorated with holly and balloons. The window curtains are open and a fire is pleasantly burning in the grate.*

(See the Ground Plan at the end of the Play.)

As the Curtain *rises "The Children's Overture" is heard.* Mary Meldon *is sitting at the writing table, writing. She is a pleasing person, completely capable of weathering the storms that, for some reason or other, appear to overtake, if not to overcome, the* Meldon *family at all-too-frequent intervals. After a few moments* Ann *comes down the stairs and enters the room. She is decidedly pretty, or at least attractive. Not in any arresting fashion, but the prettiness and the attraction are there all right. She is* Mary Meldon's *younger daughter and is a little obscured by her more dazzling sister,* Olivia. *She speaks with just the least suspicion of hesitation in her voice and is inclined to separate syllables, possibly because of this hesitation. She is becomingly dressed, is about twenty years old, and looks quite a bit younger.*

Ann (*as she enters*). Hello, Mummy! (*As she moves behind* Mary's *chair.*) *Still* writing Christmas cards on Christmas Eve?

Mary. Yes. Every year my list gets longer and longer. And every year I forget someone who always sends me one.

Ann (*picking up a Christmas card*). And then you send them a New Year's card and pretend you hadn't forgotten them. Who is this going to?

Mary. Mrs Highland.

Ann (*glancing at the card*). I don't think it's very tactful. (*She reads.*) "Wishing you all you can want in the world—and then some more."

Mary. What's wrong with that?

Ann (*dropping the card on the writing table*). She's just had twins! (*She moves above the* R. *end of the settee, turns to* Mary *and smiles.*)

Mary (*turning to* Ann). Oh, bother! It'll do for someone else.

(*She glances towards the french windows.*) Not a bit like Christmas weather, is it?

Ann (*looking towards the windows*). I think it's horrid. (*She now moves to the french windows.*) No snow. What an outlook. Daddy in bed with phlebitis.

Mary. Very unfortunate. Your Uncle Ned won't like anyone to be ill at Christmas.

Ann (*moving to the fireplace*). It takes the spotlight off *him*.

Mary. Well, if anyone *has* to be ill, Uncle Ned thinks it should be himself. And, when he finds your father in bed *and* your Aunt Topsey here—fireworks! (*She returns to her cards.*)

Ann. Uncle Ned and Aunt Topsey. Mummy, why on earth should *all* our relations be funny?

Mary (*still writing*). *Everyone's* relations are funny, but you only see the funniness in your own.

Ann. I don't know. I think ours are funnier than usual. Look at Uncle Ned.

Mary (*looking up*). I shall have to look at him for the next ten days, so why should I start before he arrives?

Ann. Of course, he's a perfect dear. But he's so ex-explos-ive. And you can never tell when the explosion's coming.

Mary (*looking round at Ann; uneasily*). I certainly wish he and your Aunt Topsey didn't fight like cat and dog on the few occasions they do meet. I'm not at all certain what he'll do when he finds she's here.

Ann (*astonished and horrified*). Mo-ther! (*She moves above the L. end of the settee.*) Haven't you told him she's with us for Christmas?

Mary. I have *not*.

Ann. It *is* going to be a happy Christmas. How a nice person like you came to have a sister like Aunt Topsey, I just don't understand.

Mary. There's nothing wrong with Aunt Topsey, if you take her the right way. There's a lot to be said for her. She . . .

Ann. Yes, she says it all for herself. (*She moves below the L. end of the settee.*)

Mary. Your aunt may be a little difficult at times, but that's because she's had an unusual life. Don't forget, she was the first woman to visit the Fiji Isles.

Ann. The Fijis won't forget it.

(Alice *enters from the hall. She is the* Meldon's *"general". Crossed in love, apparently on repeated occasions—and this is understandable, possibly, when you look at her—she views the world with a melancholy eye. She is well over forty, but would not admit that a guess in the direction might be correct.*)

Alice (*moving to L. of* Mary). I wish you'd speak to Miss Topsey—Miss Richards, ma'am.

Mary. What about, Alice?

ALICE. I bring her her morning tea at half-past seven and she goes asleep again without drinking it. Half an hour later she rings the bell and tells me her tea was brought up cold.

MARY (*hesitating*). I'm sorry, Alice.

ALICE. And, if that weren't enough, she writes notices and pins 'em up in her room—"*This* hasn't been dusted"—"*This* hasn't been swept".

ANN. Oh, dear! (*She flops on to the* L. *end of the settee.*)

ALICE. I add notices of my own now—"This isn't going to be" —"Neither is this".

MARY. I'm sorry, Alice. It's very wrong of her. I'll certainly speak to Miss Richards.

(AUNT TOPSEY *enters from the hall. She is a short, black, determined little figure, wearing a permanent frown, and has a mouth of the strength of that of a conger-eel. Her expression is always grim, and she loves battle—the bigger the odds, the better. She has a garment and knitting-needles in her hands. On seeing her,* MARY's *voice weakens and* ALICE *moves above the settee.*)

Oh—er—Topsey. We were just—er—talking about you.

TOPSEY (*moving down a few paces into the room*). Nothing good (*with a glance at* ALICE) I'll warrant.

MARY (*feebly*). Alice was just saying . . .

TOPSEY (*immediately*). She's always just saying. If she'd sometimes be just doing, this house would be the better for it.

ALICE (*indignantly*). Look here, Miss Richards . . .

TOPSEY (*making a sudden movement towards* ALICE *and glaring at her*). I'm looking! Well—what?

ALICE (*feebly*). Oh—er—Nothing.

TOPSEY. Then don't waste time talking about it. Your apron's dirty.

(*With a despairing gesture,* ALICE *quickly exits through the hall.*)

MARY (*more firmly*). Topsey, you really mustn't talk to Alice like that. You're not in Fiji now. (*She puts her cards in some envelopes.*)

TOPSEY (*turning to* MARY). Wish I was. Wouldn't have to listen to servants' impudence.

ANN (*rising*). That isn't fair! Alice never said a word.

TOPSEY. You saw what she *looked*! (*She moves to the* R. *end of the settee accusingly.*) I suppose you were putting her up to some mischief?

ANN. Oh, no! (*She moves to the fireplace.*) In-deed, no, I wasn't, Aunt Topsey.

TOPSEY (*sitting down on the settee and looking at a picture on the wall down* L. *which has mistletoe over it*). And, what's *that* stuff? Mistletoe —Ha! Wonder you don't wear it in your hat.

MARY (*striving for peace*). Ann, show your aunt the Christmas cards. (*To* TOPSEY.) There are some quite nice ones amongst them this year.

(ANN *collects a few Christmas cards from the mantelpiece and shows them to* TOPSEY, *who looks at them with an expression of utmost disparagement.*)

TOPSEY (*taking a card and peering at it*). Who's this from?—The Williamsons—"Wishing you were all with us now around the festive board". We'd be bored all right. (*She turns over the card instantly and looks at the back.*) Fourpence!

ANN (*despairingly*). This is rather sweet. (*She reads.*)

"What a sight for Christmas eyes.
Christmas turkey, pudding, pies.
These will surely bring to you . . ."

TOPSEY (*tersely*). Indigestion! Did the Clarkes send you this one?

ANN (*sitting beside* TOPSEY). Yes—a beauty.

TOPSEY (*looking at it closely*). I wonder who sent it to them. (*She picks another card and reads it.*)

(TONY *enters from the hall. He is an extremely good-looking youth of about twenty-two. Like* ANN, *he looks younger than his age. He has— when he likes—a charming, an almost irresistibly charming, manner. He is dressed a shade wildly. Green corduroys and an extravagant jacket perhaps, because* TONY *is an artist and takes himself seriously, when he remembers to do so. He has some letters in his hand.*)

TONY (*moving down a few paces into the room*). Hello, Mrs Meldon. Hello, Miss Richards.

MARY. Enjoy the tea-party, Tony?

TONY (*moving between* MARY *and* TOPSEY). Hellish! Mrs Gray at her very worst. Has she been in the Navy, or something?

MARY. The Navy! Why?

TONY. She's growing a beard.

TOPSEY. Just because you think you're going to be an artist, there's no need to forget you were once supposed to be a gentleman.

ANN. Who else was there?

TONY. That ghastly Clifton girl.

MARY. Why ghastly?

TONY. Damn it, she's biscuit-shaped.

MARY. Tony!

TONY. You know (*with a gesture*) nothing coming and nothing going.

TOPSEY (*rising*). I may be old-fashioned (*with a look at* MARY) and I may have been accustomed to the society of savages. But I will not listen to such vulgarity. I'm going to sit in the library. (*She is about to move in the direction of the door* R.)

TONY (*playfully trying to stop her*). Don't go, Miss Richards.

TOPSEY (*trying to dodge him*). Thank you! But I'm sure Ann appreciates your witticisms ... *I don't!*

TONY. But, please ...

TOPSEY (*pushing past him*). Get out of my way!

(*She exits* R.)

TONY (*looking after her*). I love my love with an F, because she's friendly. I hate her with an F, because she's fearful. I brought her to Fiji and fed her on French beans.

MARY (*laughing*). Shut up, Tony.

TONY. I've shut. (*He moves to* MARY's *chair.*) Anything for the post, Mrs Meldon?

MARY. Quite a few. Thanks. (*She hands him some envelopes.*)

TONY. I'll take the dog with me. Ann, do you know where Olivia is?

(MARY *begins to tidy the writing table.*)

ANN. No, Tony, I don't.

TONY. I want to show her some more of my sketches. (*He moves towards the arch.*)

ANN. I'm sure she'll like that. (*She returns the cards to the mantel-piece.*)

TONY (*turning at the arch*). Gosh, your sister's quick. She gets the idea the moment you show her anything. Really artistic appreciation. Never met anyone so quick in the uptake before. Phenomenal. Olivia's got a perfectly marvellous eye for line.

(TONY *exits through the hall.* ANN *watches him go.*)

ANN (*bitterly*). Olivia's got a perfectly marvellous eye for Tony.

MARY (*looking up*). I thought—I rather thought you and Tony ...

ANN. Then don't think about it an-any more, Mummy. Tony's fallen for Olivia. How could he help falling?

MARY (*turning to her*). What do you mean?

ANN (*moving below the settee*). She tripped him up.

MARY. Really, Ann! That isn't like *you.*

ANN (*in an uncertain voice*). Why should Olivia add Tony to her collection? She might have left *him* alone. Goodness knows, she's got enough fea-thers in *her* cap. (*She sits on the* L. *end of the settee.*)

MARY (*rising and moving to* ANN). Ann, darling, I didn't know— I thought Tony liked you far more than he liked Olivia. (*She sits* R. *of* ANN.)

ANN (*desperately*). So he does, Mummy—but I can't make him see it.

MARY (*sympathetically*). Oh dear.

ANN (*trying hard not to cry*). When Tony was here last month (*almost tearful now*) he did seem to be in-interested in me, although I don't understand his beastly drawings. And Olivia didn't like that. She thought everyone should be in-interested in her and no-one in *me*.

MARY (*gently*). Perhaps, if you tried to understand Tony's drawings . . .

ANN. I do try—I do! But when he shows you something that looks like an all-alligator with two tails and tells you it's an autumn afternoon in the—in the Bay of Biscay—what—what *are* you to say? (*She begins to sob a little.*)

MARY. If he has to be an artist he might try to be a sane one.

ANN. He says there's no such thing as a sane artist.

MARY. He's about right. In any case, Tony's strong line is cartoons. Why doesn't he go in for that?

ANN. He says he sees the world not as it is—but as it isn't. (*She sobs again.*)

MARY (*grimly*). It isn't only cartoonists who do that.

ANN. And I don't believe Olivia understands his pictures a little bit. It's just that she's cleverer than me.

MARY. Than *I*, dear. The verb "to be" takes the same case after it as before it.

ANN (*rising and moving to the armchair above the fireplace*). Damn the verb "to be"! (*She turns to* MARY; *still sobbing.*) And damn Tony's pictures! And damn! Damn! *Damn* Olivia. (*She dabs her eyes.*)

MARY. Ann! Really.

(ENID MARTLEY *enters from the hall. She is a good-looking woman of about fifty; rather quiet in manner, but quite capable of humour and of emotion. She is an attractive person in quite a definite degree, and she is well-dressed in a style that suits her. She is the widow of an Irish artist, who died some years ago. She is English herself but her son,* TONY, *if he has not inherited an Irish accent—thanks to the baleful influences of English preparatory and public schools—has certainly become heir to the temperament and versatility which one would expect from the son of an artist from the Better Island.*)

ENID (*taking a few paces into the room and seeing* ANN *dabbing at her eyes*). Ann, dear, whatever's wrong with your eyes?

ANN (*desperately*). Hay fever.

ENID. But, my dear child . . .

ANN. Oh!

(ANN, *still sobbing, dashes out through the door* L.)

ENID (*to* MARY). Hay fever—in December. Whatever's the matter with the girl, Mary?

MARY (*laconically*). Love! (*She rises and moves to the fireplace.*)

ENID (*moving above the* L. *end of the settee*). Love? I suppose it is like hay fever really. Comes on in the spring and there's no cure.

MARY (*arranging the cards on the mantelpiece*). I fancy it's Tony.

Enid. I shall have to speak to that son of mine. What's been happening?

Mary. Just the usual affaire, I imagine.

Enid. Having affaires is hereditary with Tony. His poor father was having one of the most hectic affaires of his life with his nurse the week he died.

Mary (*turning to* Enid; *laughing*). What a placid person you are, Enid.

Enid (*moving round to the front of the settee*). Why shouldn't I be? If one isn't able to be placid at my age, when will one? (*She sits at the* L. *end of the settee.*)

Mary. Gracious! You talk as though you were a hundred.

Enid. Do I? Well, I'm past the half-century, and I enjoy it. I think it's a pleasant age for a woman. The treacherous thirties are behind one, and the fighting forties. Horrible years, those.

Mary. Yes. No-one but a fool bewails his vanished youth once it has vanished. It's the vanishing process that hurts. But—(*looking at* Enid) for such a well-balanced person you're singularly short-sighted.

Enid. Am I? Why?

Mary. Ned Meldon.

Enid. What about poor Ned?

Mary (*taking a cigarette box from the mantelpiece*). You know perfectly well he's head over heels in love with you—always has been. (*She opens the box.*)

Enid. Ridiculous!

Mary (*offering* Enid *a cigarette*). And the poor boy just can't summon up the courage to ask you to marry him.

Enid (*taking a cigarette*). Mary, my dear! Have you been reading *Home Chat* or *Peg's Paper?*

Mary (*taking a cigarette, closing the box and returning it to the mantelpiece*). You're not going to put me off like that. (*She takes a box of matches from the mantelpiece.*) Ned's coming here today. You've just got to help him to say what he wants to. (*She offers* Enid *a light and lights her own cigarette.*) It's your fault. You're too lazy to make an effort, so you just do nothing and hope that Ned will.

Enid (*puffing out a cloud of smoke and laughing*). Hope?

Mary (*replacing the box of matches on the mantelpiece*). Yes. (*She sits on the* R. *arm of the armchair above the fireplace.*) Even at your great age, hope springs eternal in the human breast.

Enid. Possibly. But the springs are getting a bit rusty.

Mary. Enid, I could shake you.

Enid. You couldn't. Not on that conviction, my dear.

(Olivia *enters from the door* R. *She is rather tall and decidedly commanding. She affects the dramatic style of dress to match her dramatic voice and manner. Unlike her younger sister,* Ann, *there is no hesitation in her speech—none whatever. She has a lovely voice and she uses it with effect.*)

Olivia (*moving* r.c.). Anyone seen Tony?

Mary. He's just gone to post some letters, Olivia. He'll be back in a moment.

Olivia. Glaston's have sent the Santa Claus costume, Mother.

Mary. Oh! I wonder, could we persuade your Uncle Ned to play Father Christmas in your father's place for the convalescent kids? (*To* Enid.) At the Home next door, you know. They'll be so disappointed if . . .

Olivia (*moving to the* r. *end of the settee*). Uncle Ned will be far better as the Demon King. And, speaking of demons, Enid, you'd better look out. Aunt Topsey's out gunning for you.

Enid. For me? Good gracious! What have I done?

Olivia. She says you've taken the bedroom she's always been given before.

Enid. For heaven's sake, Mary, let me move. I don't mind in the slightest where I sleep.

Mary. How ridiculous of her. Where is she, Olivia? (*She rises.*)

Olivia. She's in the library, knitting garments for the Zulus, or something, (*to* Enid) and looking as though she'd like to get those needles into you.

Mary (*to* Enid; *crossing to the door,* r.). Come on, my dear. Let's go and talk to her together. If you tell her you'd prefer the room she's in now, nothing will persuade her to leave it.

(Mary *exits through the door* r.)

Enid (*rising and following* Mary *to the door*). You mean, let's go and listen to her? (*To* Olivia.) Oh, dear. I do wish your Aunt Topsey didn't hate me so much.

Olivia (*moving to* Enid). Don't worry. She hates every one except herself, and she's not too keen on her. The truth of it is, Aunt Topsey is an old . . .

Enid (*interfering*). I know—second letter of the alphabet.

(*She exits* r. Olivia *smiles and goes to the mirror at the fireplace. She is looking at herself with no little satisfaction, when* Tony *enters from the hall.*)

Tony (*seeing her*). Stop! Don't move.

Olivia (*without turning*). Why, Tony?

Tony (*moving down stage a few paces*). I could draw you like that.

Olivia. Oh! I don't think I'd care for a back view of me.

Tony (*taking a step towards her*). But your back is so full of character. When I do portraits, I shall always do back views. People say character lies in the face. (*Wildly.*) Olivia—there's more character in the curve of your spine—in the contour of your back —your back . . .

Olivia (*turning round quickly*). Don't finish it, Tony. You artists are so dreadfully anatomical. (*She moves to the* l. *end of the settee.*) Is there something so terribly wrong with my face?

Tony (*moving to her above the settee*). It's a beautiful face—a face that would launch a thousand ships.

Olivia. Like Helen?

Tony. Like Hell—and Helen—Olivia—(*he moves nearer to her*) —you're . . .

Olivia (*gently fending him off and moving* R.C.). Don't be fickle, Tony. You know it's Ann who really interests you.

Tony (*turning; taken aback*). Ann? Ann's a nice child, but . . .

Olivia. But you like nice children.

Tony. When you're about, Ann doesn't even exist to me.

Olivia (*moving to the* R. *end of the settee*). That isn't very nice of you, Tony. After all, you and Ann used to be great pals.

Tony (*very impressed*). That's just like you, Olivia. You're so— so big-minded. (*He pauses.*) I say Ann's lucky to have a sister like you. (*He moves round to just below the* L. *end of the settee.*) I hope she realizes it.

Olivia. She realizes it all right.

Tony (*moving a step nearer to her*). Ann's O.K. in her way. But she doesn't know the first thing about art. *You're* altogether different—you're wonderful. You've got depth and perspective, Olivia. I want to do a painting of you.

Olivia (*moving to the table down* L). Perhaps I'll let you some day. (*She picks up a sheet of paper from the table.*) What's this?

Tony (*moving down to the table and looking at the paper with her*). Oh, just a cartoon I've done of Uncle Ned.

Olivia (*sitting at the* R. *end of the settee*). You've certainly got a lovely subject. Oh, Tony. (*She laughs.*) It's wizard! It's a perfect marvel. He'd explode if he saw it. Why don't you go in for cartoons? You'd make a fortune.

Tony (*taking the cartoon and putting it on the mantelpiece*). Don't want to waste my time on tripe like that. (*He moves back to her.*) Look here, Olivia. (*He sits beside her.*) You know—you know how much I—like you—don't you?

Olivia. Well—I didn't really—do you?

Tony. Good Lord! You know I do—I can't believe it. It's all too wonderful—too marvellous—that you should let me be a friend of yours.

Olivia. It's wonderful of *you*, Tony.

Tony. We speak the same language, don't we?

Olivia. The same language, Tony.

Tony. Olivia!

(*He is just about to take her in his arms when* Ann *enters* L. Tony *and* Olivia *quickly sit apart.*)

Ann (*seeing them as they move away*). Well, I've broken that up, anyway. (*She moves* L.C.)

(Tony *rises and moves down* L.)

Olivia (*rising and moving above the* R. *end of the settee*). Hello, Ann. I've got a nice little job for you.

Ann (*sadly*). You seem to have got a nice little job for *yourself*.

Olivia. Those parcels for the Children's Home have got to be tied up. I've done all the names and labels.

Ann. Where are the beastly things?

Olivia (*sweetly*). In the library. You'll be able to talk to Aunt Topsey while you're doing them.

Ann. That's very thoughtful of you.

Tony (*looking extremely uncomfortable*). Look here—I'll get them for you. (*He moves* R.C.)

Ann. That would be very n-nice of you, Tony.

Tony (*turning to them*). In the library, you said?

Olivia. How sweet of you, Tony. Thanks ever so much.

(Tony *exits hastily through the door* R.)

Ann (*moving to the fireplace*). Olivia, you're a greedy beast. Couldn't you let me have even *him*?

Olivia (*moving to the writing table and taking a cigarette out of the box*). Don't be a silly child.

Ann. I'm not silly, and I'm not a child. Why can't you leave Tony alone?

Olivia (*picking up a box of matches*). Leave Tony alone? Well, I do like that. Since when has he become your exclusive property? (*She lights her cigarette and replaces the matches.*)

Ann. He isn't my exclusive property. But why must you take him away from me? You've got dozens and dozens of men friends, haven't you?

Olivia (*moving above the settee; smiling*). Dozens and dozens.

Ann. And yet you must . . .

Olivia. You haven't got the right idea at all, my dear. You see, the trouble is you don't understand Tony.

Ann. And you do, I suppose?

Olivia (*with satisfaction*). I think so. (*She moves below the* L. *end of the settee.*)

Ann. That's your big act, isn't it? Understanding men . . . And I know you don't really like Tony. It only just pleases your vanity to take him away from me.

Olivia (*moving to the* R. *end of the settee*). You mustn't talk such nonsense. (*She sits at the* R. *end of the settee.*) In the first place I *do* like Tony and, in the second, I can't help him falling for me, can I?

Ann (*moving below the* L. *end of the settee*). And, of course, you've never thrown yourself in his way, have you?

OLIVIA. Certainly not!

ANN. No . . . (*She moves to the french windows.*) You just happen always to *be* there at the right mo-ment. It's very clever of you—it must take a lot of prac-tice.

(MARY *enters* R. *followed by* TONY.)

OLIVIA. Thank you, dear, you're quite right, it does. Tony's just perfect to practise on.

ANN (*turning to her*). Ooh! I think you're per-fectly horrid.

MARY. What are you two quarreling about?

ANN (*with a look at* TONY). Nothing of the—the slightest im-portance.

TONY (*catching the look*). Oh—thanks. (*He rapidly turns to exit* R.)

MARY (*stopping him*). No! I want your assistance, Tony. (*She crosses above the settee to the fireplace.*) And yours, you two.

OLIVIA. Whatever's happened now?

MARY (*idly taking up the caricature of* NED *from the mantelpiece*). Oh, Tony! How utterly wicked of you. (*She looks at the cartoon and laughs.*)

OLIVIA. It's terrific, isn't it?

(ANN *moves between the armchair and the settee.*)

MARY. It *will* be terrific if Uncle Ned sees it. (*She carelessly replaces the cartoon.*) Now, listen to me, all of you. (*To* ANN *and* OLIVIA.) You see your Aunt Topsey isn't—well, she isn't in very good form.

TONY (*moving to the* R. *end of the settee*). Good form? She seems fighting fit. (*He sits on the* R. *arm of the settee.*)

MARY. I mean—she's rather put out. Well—she's in a very bad temper, if you prefer.

OLIVIA. Aunt Topsey by any name would smell as sweet.

MARY. Uncle Ned has no idea she is with us for Christmas. I'm afraid he'll be boiling when he finds her here.

OLIVIA. What do you want us to do, Mother?

MARY. All I want is the opportunity to have a talk with your Uncle Ned before *he* sees Topsey.

OLIVIA. To break it to him?

MARY. Well—er—yes.

OLIVIA. How will you put it to him, mother?

MARY. I'll—I'll appeal to his Christmas spirit.

ANN (*crossing behind the settee to the chair* R.). I'm afraid Uncle Ned's Christmas spirit will be very fiery.

MARY. I'll have to take that risk. All I ask is that one of you keeps Aunt Topsey busy until I get a chance to talk to Ned. (*She looks at them.*) *You'll* do that for me, Ann?

ANN. But I . . . (*She sits in the chair.*) Why is it when there's a dir-dirty job to be done everyone always picks on me?

MARY. Just sit and talk to your aunt. And keep her in the

library when Ned arrives. With your uncle so much depends on
things going right at the start. If he begins to get ruffled . . .

TONY (*rising and moving up* R.). You needn't worry, Ann. It's
a soft job this time. Your Aunt Topsey's sitting there like a cross
between the Rock of Gibraltar and the Hallelujah Chorus.

ANN. But supposing she doesn't want to stay in the library?

TONY (*moving down to* R. *of* ANN). Oh, in that case you'll have to
persuade her to. Try a hammer——

(TOPSEY *enters* R. *unnoticed by* TONY *or* ANN.)

—or give her a bone to chew.

(OLIVIA *rises and moves to* MARY, *both making frantic gestures to* TONY
to try and stop him.)

ANN. A bone?

TONY (*noticing* OLIVIA'S *gestures*). Olivia, have you got St Vitus
dance? (*To* ANN; *easily.*) Yes. Give her a bone—a human bone.
I've often suspected that your Aunt Topsey *ate* men.

MARY. Tony!

TOPSEY (*quickly moving above the settee and speaking with vigour*).
If she couldn't find a better man than you, she'd stay hungry.

(TONY *and* ANN *turn round aghast.* ANN *rises.* TONY *wilts.*)

MARY. Topsey!

TOPSEY. It's not my fault, if I come into a room and find you all
talking about me behind my back, is it?

OLIVIA. Aunt Topsey!

TOPSEY. Oh, I know. You needn't tell me what's in your mind.
This isn't *my* house. If it *was*, there'd be a lot of things different
from what they are now.

TONY. I'm sure of that.

TOPSEY (*quickly*). And you'd be one of them.

(TONY *moves up stage a little.* ANN *sits in the chair.*)

MARY. Well, Topsey, I'm sorry about . . .

TOPSEY. My room? (*She moves* L. *below the settee.*) Oh, it doesn't
matter, *of course.* If you like to put me in the attic, facing north . . .

ANN (*rising*). But you're not in an attic—and you're not facing
north.

(OLIVIA *moves behind the settee to* TONY.)

TOPSEY. My room's at the top of the house, isn't it? If that
isn't an attic, I'd like to know what is. And, if it doesn't face
north, then the sun must have started rising in the west. (*She sits
in the centre of the settee.*)

MARY. Well, if you feel like that, we'll certainly move you.

TOPSEY. No, thank you. (*With immense resignation.*) I believe
in taking what I'm given without complaining.

MARY. Very well, my dear. (*Tactfully, as she moves to* L.C.) Oh, by the way, the children next door are singing carols tonight. You'll come, won't you, Topsey?

TOPSEY. I suppose I shall have to. I don't like children, especially *slum* children.

TONY (*moving down to the* R. *of the settee*).

"The children of the poor,
I really can't endure.

(MARY *signals him to stop.*)

I have to close
My Roman nose
They smell so like manure."

(*He makes the appropriate gesture.*)

TOPSEY. I suppose you think that's clever?

TONY (*airily*). Not at all—a child could do it.

TOPSEY (*shortly*). A child did!

OLIVIA (*moving to the radiogram, picking up the box of chocolates and offering them to* TOPSEY *over the back of the settee*). Will you have a chocolate, Auntie?

TOPSEY. Don't eat chocolates!

TONY (*taking out his cigarette-case and offering* TOPSEY *a cigarette*). Have a cigarette?

TOPSEY. Don't smoke cigarettes.

TONY. Gracious! What *do* you do? (*He moves below the writing table.*) All right! Question withdrawn. Don't tell me.

OLIVIA. How are you getting on with the Hottentots' Chilprufes?

TOPSEY. I don't know what you mean! I'm knitting knickers.

TONY. Knitting knickers! (*In horror.*) Purling panties, please!

(ALICE *enters from the hall and moves down* L. *a few paces.*)

TOPSEY. And they're not for Hottentots. Hottentots don't wear knickers.

TONY. Then how do they keep hot and tot?

MARY (*crossing to* ALICE). Yes, Alice?

ALICE. Mr Edwards phoned, ma'am—from the station—he's waiting for a taxi.

MARY. Thanks, Alice.

(ALICE *exits through the hall.* MARY *looks significantly at* ANN.)

He'll be along in just a few minutes. (*She moves down to the* L. *of* ANN.) Won't he, Ann, dear? (*She moves above* ANN.)

TOPSEY (*settling herself more comfortably and looking at* OLIVIA *and* ANN). Well, which of you two girls is running after *him* (*with a gesture at* TONY) *now?*

OLIVIA. Really, Aunt Topsey. (*She moves to the* R. *of the armchair above the fireplace.*)

TOPSEY. Brr! Girls these days have no shame. If I wanted a husband I wouldn't behave like a cat stalking a mouse. I'd try . . .

TONY (*interrupting very politely*). St Dunstan's?

MARY. Tony! (*She moves above the* R. *end of the settee.*) Ann, darling, didn't you say you wanted to talk to your Aunt Topsey?

ANN (*blankly*). No.

MARY. Yes, dear. Didn't you want to ask her some questions about Fiji? (*She moves to the window and looks out* R.)

TOPSEY (*showing interest*). It's about time someone showed some interest in someone else as well as themselves. What did you want to know?

ANN (*slowly rising*). Well, I don't know that there was anything in particular. (*She moves to the* R. *end of the settee; weakly.*) Just about Fiji. (*She sits* R. *of* TOPSEY.)

TONY (*moving to the radiogram*). And the Fiji-gees!

(OLIVIA *sits in the armchair above the fireplace.*)

TOPSEY (*glaring at* TONY). Well, I suppose if anyone knows about the Islands it should be me. I was the first white woman to land there—in—I forget the year.

(*The others look at each other in despair, for* TOPSEY *looks as though she meant to make a job of it.* TONY *picks up the ukelele from the top of the radiogram and examines it.*)

ANN (*interrupting*). There's a picture in the library. Shall we have a look at it there while you tell me about it?

TOPSEY. No, fetch it here.

(TONY *moves with the ukelele above the chair* R.)

OLIVIA. But they gave you a friendly reception, didn't they?

TOPSEY. Yes, very. As I was getting ready to step off the steamer, the Paramount Chief arrived to welcome me.

(TONY *very gently strikes a few chords.*)

The Chief said, in Fijian dialect: "Hail! Hail! Hail!"

(*The moment she has spoken,* TONY *strikes three low ,loud, similar chords on the ukelele.*)

(*She shows her annoyance and looks round.*) The Paramount Chief had his little daughter with him. She raised her hand in greeting and said . . .

(TONY *immediately strikes three very high notes on the ukelele.*)

TOPSEY (*turning round*). If you don't want to listen, perhaps you'll kindly leave the room?

(MARY *signals to* ANN *to get rid of* TOPSEY.)

TONY. Please, teacher. (*He puts up his hand.*) May I . . . ?

(*With a wink at* ANN, TONY *exits* R.)

MARY (*moving down to the* L. *of the settee*). Well—Alice will be turning us out if we don't move.

(OLIVIA *rises and stands with her back to the fireplace.*)

TOPSEY. Nonsense! There's lots of time yet. Of course, if you don't want me to tell you about . . .

MARY. Of course we do. But, you see . . .

TOPSEY. Very well, then. Well, we landed, and what did we find? Conditions on the Islands baffled description. There was no indoor sanitation and the outdoor sanitation was very outdoor.

(*There is the sound of a car driving up to the front door.* MARY *goes to the window again and looks out, and then turns into the room again and nods despairingly at* OLIVIA.)

The natives live in mudhuts . . .

ANN (*rising*). There's a wonderful picture of a mud hut in the library.

(MARY *begins to make despairing gestures to the others.*)

TOPSEY (*paying no attention*). Mud huts, which were made of adobe. The customs of the natives were really too . . .

(MARY *is still making gestures at the others when the door,* R., *opens, and* TONY *enters and moves to* R.C. *He is carrying some strange woollen garments in his hands.*)

MARY. Tony! What *have* you got there? (*She moves below the radiogram.*)

(TONY *waves the garments in the air.* TOPSEY *turns round with a sudden movement, rises and rushes to* TONY.)

TOPSEY (*to* TONY). My knickers! (*She snatches the knitting from him.*)

(OLIVIA *takes a step forward.*)

TONY (*looking accusingly at* ANN). It's that dog of yours, Ann.

(ANN *moves quickly below the chair* R., *looking at* TONY.)

The place is a shambles. There are garments everywhere—all over the place.

TOPSEY (*to* ANN). Has your dog got into the library?

TONY. He has. And he's run amok amongst the hottentotities, the dirty dog.

ANN. I—I never . . .

MARY (*as she moves to the window*). Quick, Topsey, dear. You'd better go and see what damage has been done. (*She looks out of the window.*) Another moment and it may be too late.

TOPSEY (*moving to the door* R.). Is that dog still there?

TONY. Good Lord, yes. He's having the time of his young life. There won't be a purl left if you don't hurry.

TOPSEY. Done on purpose. (*To* ANN.) Come with me. Come here at once.

(*She talks herself out* R.)

MARY (*moving above the settee*). Better go. *Quick, Ann.* Uncle Ned's in the hall.

ANN (*moving to the door* R.). Why—why—why is it always *me?*

(*She exits* R.)

MARY. Thank God for that dog.

TONY. There isn't a dog. (*He moves to the* R. *of the settee and announces dramatically.*) I'm the dog!

MARY. You mean? *Oh,* you darling boy. (*She pauses.*) Oh, good heavens!

(ENID *enters* R.)

Where's the whisky and soda? *Where's* the whisky and soda?

ENID (*indicating it on the table up* R.). It's here, dear. (*She moves between the chair and the settee.*)

(OLIVIA *takes the little table from down* L. *and puts it in front of the arm-chair above the fireplace. This is for* UNCLE NED. *On the table she puts an ashtray and some matches.*)

MARY. Uncle Ned's so difficult. If you don't ask him to have a drink he's annoyed. If you do offer him one, he asks you if you think he's a drunkard. What *is* one to do?

TONY (*laconically*). Don't risk it. Offer him a drink! (*He moves down* R.)

MARY (*moving* L.C.). He seems to be a long time in the hall.

ENID (*crossing to the fireplace to tidy her hair in the mirror*). What are we all doing *here?* We should go out to meet him, shouldn't we?

OLIVIA. Lord, no! He *hates* being met.

TONY. I think you all get yourselves in a flap about Uncle Ned. All you've got to do is to keep calm and remember he's jet-propelled.

OLIVIA. Jet-propelled? Hell-propelled.

MARY (*moving below the* L. *end of the settee*). Whatever *is* keeping him?

(ALICE *enters from the hall. She is looking shaken and seems to find it hard to say what she wants.* OLIVIA *moves above the upstage armchair.*)

Well, Alice?

ALICE (*moving a few paces into the room*). Mr Ned's here, ma'am.

He's in *very, very* good spirits. (*She looks round tragically at the others.*)
     Mary. What *do* you mean?
     Alice. He—he kissed me.
     Tony. He *must* be in good spirits.
     Mary. Yes. But where *is* he? Where is he?
     Alice (*with hesitation*). He's gone to the—to the . . .
     Mary. To the what?
     Alice. To the cloakroom, ma'am.
     Mary. My God! And the paint's still wet! (*She rushes to the arch-way.*)
     Tony (*stopping her*). Hold on!
     Mary. Get out of my way, Tony.
     Tony. I'll go. This is a job for a man. (*He moves towards the arch-way.*)

(Alice *eases to the* r. Olivia *laughs and moves a little away from the armchair towards the* r.)

     Mary (*moving below the settee*). For heaven's sake, quick! Quick! He'll be raging if . . . (*She suddenly stops.*)

(Uncle Ned *enters from the hall and* Tony *drops back to* r. *of the archway.* Uncle Ned *is of medium size, possibly rather small. His hair is thinning. He is a clean-shaven, good-looking man, with a very charming smile. Rather military in his general appearance. His face is a little florid and its rather high colour tends to show up his alert and in- telligent eyes. At the moment,* Mary's *fears appear to be groundless, for he seems to be radiantly happy. He stands in the archway for a moment, beaming at everyone.*)

     Ned (*fruitily and heartily*). Happy Christmas! (*He advances into the room towards* Mary.)

          (Mary *moves towards* Ned *and they meet above the settee.*)

Ah, Mary! Mary! (*He takes her in his arms and kisses her heartily.*)
     Mary. Dear Ned.

          (Alice *exits through the hall.* Tony *moves* l. *of the chair.*)

     Ned (*holding* Mary *and looking at her*). Not a day older. Not a wrinkle, not a crow's-foot, not a line. "Mary had a little lamb." (*He moves to* Olivia.) What a lovely little lamb! (*He embraces her.*) Not married yet? 'Pon my word, some foolish fellow's missing his chances! (*He notices* Enid.) And (*releasing her*) if it isn't my dear old friend. (*He moves to* Enid.) What a sight for sore eyes she is.
     Enid. Hello, Ned, dear.

(Ned *takes her hands, but holds her at arm's length. She is quite uncertain whether he's going to kiss her or not. He looks at her in great admiration.*)

     Ned (*very sentimentally*). Between such old friends as us, there's only one possible greeting.

(ENID *comes forward, but* NED *lets one of her hands go and raises the other to his lips with old-world gallantry.*)

Dear—*dear* lady.

(ENID *smiles, amused at him.*)

(*He turns and sees* TONY.) And how's Tony? (*He moves towards* TONY *below the settee and takes his hand, giving it a terrific squeeze.*) Grand to see you, old boy. *Grand!*

TONY. Grand to see you, Uncle Ned. You—er—feel very fit. (*He looks ruefully at his hand.*)

NED (*surveying* TONY *and giving a sudden guffaw*). And *what* are you dressed up as—*The Green Goddess?*

TONY (*taken aback*). Dressed up as . . . ?

NED. Your coat, lad. Your trousers. (*He turns away from* TONY *and moves to* ENID.) Young people nowadays have to dress up like freaks to draw attention to themselves.

TONY (*with a bitter look*). Freaks!

NED (*instantly charming*). Don't be hurt, lad. I forgot you're an artist. You have to wear the uniform—eh?

TONY (*sitting in the chair*). Uniform!

NED (*to* ENID). We didn't need any flipperies to make people look at us, did we? Lord, I remember calling in to see you before you went to Court to be presented. That must be (*he thinks*) twenty—thirty—thirty-five years ago.

ENID. Oh, no, Ned. Not quite so long ago as *that*.

NED. And what a lovely figure you were. (*He pauses; sentimentally.*) Good heavens! I can see you now in that lovely white dress and the diamonds round your neck. Like a white swan you were. (*He moves between* MARY *and* OLIVIA.) Wasn't she, Mary?

MARY. She was.

NED (*turning to* OLIVIA). And here's another of 'em, another beauty. Heigh-ho. I'm a sentimental old fool, and every dog has his day.

MARY. You haven't had all your days yet, Ned.

NED (*moving to the armchair above the fireplace; with a laugh*). Nor all my nights—eh? (*He sits in the armchair.*)

(MARY *moves to the* R. *end of the settee and sits on the arm.* OLIVIA *moves to the settee and sits at the* L. *end.* ENID *sits in the armchair down* L.)

Here's the old gentleman's armchair all ready for him. (*He takes a pipe, tobacco pouch and matches from his pocket.*) And a table for all his litter. (*Suddenly.*) Where's John?

MARY (*a little nervously*). Poor John's got phlebitis. He isn't allowed out of bed.

NED. Phlebitis? What! Is he *ill?*

MARY. No, but he can't put his leg to the ground.

NED. Never heard such nonsense in my life. Old fusspot! Who's his doctor?

OLIVIA. Dr Gray.

NED. Old quack! I wouldn't trust him with my corns. Sorry about John, but I don't expect it's anything. He's as strong as a horse. (*He pauses.*) Wish *I* had *his* constitution. (*He sighs anxiously.*) Beginning to feel my years now.

TONY (*rising*). Nonsense, Uncle Ned. (*He moves above the settee.*) You look in the pink.

NED (*warming up a little*). What I look and what I feel are two totally different matters. (*He puts his pipe in his mouth and hurriedly takes it out again.*) No—I can't smoke. (*He looks depressed.*)

MARY. Why not, Ned?

NED (*rubbing his lips*). I'm getting shingles—shingles on my lips —felt it coming on in the train. (*He rubs his lips again.*)

MARY. These cold spots are beastly, aren't they?

NED. Cold spots! Who said anything about cold spots? Herpes Febrilis—shingles—that's what I'm getting.

MARY. But, Ned, I've got a perfectly *wonderful* cure for that.

NED. Have you now? Have you?

MARY. It's a white lipstick—Lanoline or something. You just rub it on, and . . .

NED. Are you suggesting I should use lipstick? What do you think I am?—A pansy?

MARY. But it's *white!* You can't *see* it. It's invisible.

NED. And you say it stops 'em?

MARY. It's wonderful.

NED. Then I'll try it.

MARY (*rising*). I'll get you some.

NED. No hurry! No hurry!

MARY (*sitting at the R. end of the settee*). And you'll have a tiny whisky and soda now?

(OLIVIA *rises, moves to the table up* R. *and pours out a drink for* NED.)

NED. What's that?

OLIVIA. It'd be good for you.

NED (*directly and angrily*). I suppose you imagine—I suppose you *all* believe I can't *live* without a whisky every half-hour of the day? Dammit! What do you think I am—a drunkard?

MARY (*quietly*). No, of course not, Ned. But you must be tired after your long journey. Was the train well up to time?

NED (*happily diverted again*). One minute twenty-five seconds late starting. One minute twenty-five seconds, mark you.

TONY (*moving above the* L. *end of the settee*). Gosh!

NED. Picked it up between here and Golding.*

TONY. Hot work.

NED. Lost it again at Ravelstoke Junction.*

(OLIVIA *moves towards* NED *with the drink.*)

---

* The names of local stations should be used.

Tony. Hell!

Ned. One minute, twenty-five seconds late. Lost another thirty seconds there and arrived here . . .

(Olivia *hands him the drink.*)

Thank you, Olivia, just a small one.

(Olivia *leans on the back of* Ned's *armchair.*)

Arrived here only half a minute after time. (*Triumphantly.*) How's that?

Tony. Great!

Ned (*suddenly bounding from the armchair and standing with his back to the fireplace*). Lord! But it's good to be here amongst you all. (*He thinks for a moment.*) But there's a fly in the amber. (*He moves to the* L. *of* Tony.) Where's Ann?

Mary. Oh, she's—she's in the library.

Ned. In the library! In the library! And she didn't come in to see me. Dammit! That's a nice way to be treated by one's god-daughter.

Mary. Well, you see, there was a job—in the library—she had to—to . . .

Tony (*leaning over the back of the settee; to* Mary). Hold down? (*He moves to the chair, swinging it round to face them and sits.*)

Ned. And the little beauty wouldn't leave it. Quite right, too. I'll go and find her in the library. (*He is about to move* R.)

Mary (*rising*). Oh, *no*—no!

Olivia (*moving quickly to the door* R.). I'll go and get her.

Ned. Well—well—that's good of you, Olivia.

(Olivia *exits* R.)

And we're going to hear the kiddies next door sing carols, aren't we? Grand! That will be grand.

Mary. Uncle Ned—we wondered—you know the children at the Convalescent Home next door always have a Christmas tree on Christmas Day? And John was going to be Father Christmas and distribute the presents from the tree tomorrow. Now, of course, he can't. We wondered if you . . . ? (*She crosses to the fire-place and gesticulates to* Enid *to make the request.*)

Enid. If *you* would be Father Christmas?

Ned (*frowning and moving below the* L. *end of the settee; looking at* Enid). Would *you* like me to?

Enid. I'd *love* you to.

Ned (*moving to the* R. *end of the settee; with great gusto*). Then I *will*! Damned if I don't. (*He moves above the settee.*) Love to help the kiddies. What have you got? Red cloak, long beard, sack on my shoulder?

Mary. Yes, we've got everything.

Ned (*with a gesture to a long and imaginary beard*). Then here's your

Father Christmas. (*He thinks.*) Sorry for old John, you know, but damned if I don't think I'll make a better hand at the job than he would—far better. Come on. Let's try the costume on. (*He moves R.C., facing the door R.*) By jove! I'll make a fine Santa Claus.

(ANN *enters* R.)

And *here's* the other little lamb. Come here, lambkin. (*He opens his arms.*)

(ANN *rushes into them.* NED *swings* ANN *round to the* R. *end of the settee.*)

ANN. Hel-lo, Un-cle Ned.

NED (*kissing her*). What a big little lamb it's grown into. Dammit! Olivia'll have to look to her laurels. (*Looking at* ANN *again.*) Bless you—you're prettier than ever.

ANN. You're looking very well yourself, Uncle Ned.

NED (*pleased*). Do you think so? *Do* you think so?

ANN. Why, you look *years* younger.

NED (*in high delight*). Do you hear her? (*To the others.*) Did you hear *that?* Well (*in great delight*) I'll tell you my recipe for keeping young. (*He moves behind the settee.*)

MARY (*moving to the* L. *end of the settee*). I'd like to hear it. (*She sits on the settee.*)

NED. Three rules. (*He looks benignly round at them.*) Early hours— Good whisky—And (*he pauses impressively*) *never* losing my temper.

(*There is a rather embarrassed silence after this disclosure.*)

MARY (*feebly*). I'm sure you don't find that difficult, Uncle Ned?

NED (*moving to the mantelpiece; impressively*). Easy as pie. And it's the real secret. (*He smiles tranquilly at the others, and then his eye glances at the clock.*) Mary!

MARY. Yes?

NED (*crossing to the fireplace*). That clock of yours isn't going. (*He looks at the clock on the mantelpiece carefully.*) Wants winding as usual, I expect. Where's the key? Ah! (*He sees the cartoon, takes it in his hand and studies it. He looks very angry and there is murder in his voice.*) And who does this represent, may I ask?

(ANN *moves to* TONY. ENID *rises.*)

I asked who this represents. (*He looks round the room, then glares at* TONY.) Well?

TONY (*rising; petrified*). I—I don't know . . .

NED (*his voice quivering with rage*). A caricature of a man with a nose like a strawberry—and the stomach—the stomach of a spider! (*Unconsciously his hand slides down the front of his waistcoat, fearing that it will encounter the worst.*) Who is this supposed to be?

TONY. No-one. No-one in particular.

NED. It is labelled—(*He pauses*) *Edward in Eruption.*

Tony (*fearfully*). I didn't think . . .

Ned (*throwing restraint to the winds and moving behind the settee*). You didn't think—you couldn't-think. You haven't anything to think with. You're an impertinent little whipper-snapper, and if I wasn't afraid of breaking you I'd put you across my knee and smack your bottom.

Enid. Oh, Ned. Really! I'm sure Tony . . .

Ned (*wildly*). *Bottom—bottom—bottom*! That's what I said. (*To* Tony.) And it's a pity you're too old to get yours warmed for you. Mr Clever Artistic Martley exercising his wits on a visitor in someone else's house. Very nice. Very nice. Very nice indeed.

Mary (*moving towards* Ned *a little*). If you'd only let us explain . . .

(Enid *moves to* Mary.)

Ned (*drowning her voice*). Don't interrupt me! Am I never going to be allowed to speak in this house?

Ann (*moving* R. *of* Ned). But, Uncle Ned . . .

Ned (*thrusting the picture at her*). Look at it! Look at it!

Ann (*glancing at him and venturing all on a throw*). But I think it's very funny.

Ned (*really appalled*). Funny! *You* think it funny? Have I a face like that? Have I a nose like that? Have I—(*His hand anxiously, if unobtrusively, investigates his waistcoat again.*) have I a *figure* like that.

Ann. Of course, you haven't, Uncle Ned.

Ned (*still boiling*). Then, what—what do you mean?

Ann. Well, don't you see, Uncle Ned? Tony has deliberately given you all the things you *haven't* got. That's why it *is* funny. Can't you see?

Ned (*uncompromisingly*). No!

Ann. Well—he's given you a red nose, when you have a most beaut-tiful complexion. And a fat little tummy, when everybody notices your milit-tary figure. And—and an angry face, because you're never angry.

Ned. What's that?

Ann. You nev-ver *are* angry. You just pretend to be.

(Ned *wavers, and is lost.*)

Ned (*laughing with great confidence*). Well—upon my word and honour. If that isn't very, very clever of you, Ann. Ha! (*With rising confidence.*) Had you all, that time, didn't I? You thought I *was* angry. All except little Ann. (*He laughs with much greater confidence now.*) Made you look so foolish, eh!

(Mary *and* Enid *register staggered relief.*)

(*He claps* Tony *heartily on the back.*) Damn good, my boy. Damn good.

(Ann, *relieved, moves to the window.* Enid *signals* Mary *to sit in the armchair down* L. Enid *sits on the arm* L. *beside* Mary.)

Tony (*staggered*). I'm glad!—I'm glad you like it, Uncle Ned. (*He sits in the chair.*)
Ned. Like it! It's magnificent! (*He moves above the* R. *end of the settee.*) So you all thought I'd lost my temper. This isn't the time for losing tempers—not at this season of all seasons.

(Topsey *enters through the door* R. *carrying her bag.*)

Not when we are a happy family like this without a discordant note. (*He smiles at them.*) Christmas comes but once a year. And when it comes it brings good—good . . . (*He hears the door close and turns* R. *and sees* Topsey.) Good God!

(*All look at each other in consternation.*)

Topsey (*moving* R.C.; *instantly*). Blasphemy!

(*For a moment it seems uncertain whether* Ned *will explode. Then, to everybody's astonishment, he moves to* Topsey *and embraces her.*)

Ned. Happy Christmas to my old Fijian lullaby.
Mary. I can't bear this much longer.
Topsey. You're very free with your kisses, Ned Meldon.
Ned (*delighted*). I couldn't resist the like of your sweet self, could I now?
Mary (*about to rise*). If we're going to the carols . . .

(Enid *rises,* Ann *moves to the* L. *end of the settee.*)

Ned. Of course we are. And Aunt Topsey's going to sit next to me.
Topsey. No, she isn't. You might *sing.* (*She takes a card from her bag.*)
Ned. Of course I will. Isn't that what you go to carols for?
Enid. It will be nice hearing you singing "Peace on Earth", Ned.
Topsey (*looking at the card*). They seem to have asked a lot of people—I'm forty-three.
Ned (*delightedly*). No, you're not—not by twenty years.
Mary (*rising*). Well, come along, everybody. Is it still raining?
Tony. No, it's fine now.
Ned (*moving to the Christmas tree*). Ah, we don't get the old-fashioned Christmas these days. White snow and blue noses, eh, Topsey?
Topsey. Ridiculous! Wasting time listening to those children. (*She moves* R. *of the Christmas tree.*)

Tony (*rising*)

> "The children of the poor
> Are carolling next door;
> Each little brat
> Sings three tones flat,
> I hate it all, I'm sure!"

(*He has deliberately distorted the word door to rhyme with poor.*)

Ned (*with a laugh*). A poet! Well done, Tony. Now (*with a comprehensive glance at the others*) you wouldn't think your old Uncle Ned was a poet? (*He moves down behind the settee.*) I made one up the other day. (*After some little preparation.*)

> "There was a young fellow called Ned ...

Mary (*moving below the settee towards the archway; warningly*). Uncle Ned, please.
Ned (*starting again defiantly*).

> "There was a young fellow called Ned,
> Who said as he got into bed,
> You may think I'm old-fashioned,
> But when I'm impassioned ..."

(*He pauses and looks round the room.*) No, you're too young to hear the last line. (*He moves towards the hall.*)
Mary. Just as well we are.
Ned. "Heaven pity the woman I wed."

(Mary *makes a wild dash at him and* Ned *exits precipitately to the hall.*)

Tony (*rising*). Lovely!
Mary. The wretch! Come along all of you. Come along, Topsey.

(Mary *and* Topsey *exit through the hall.* Enid *moves in front of the settee and is about to follow* Mary. Ann *moves to the fireplace.*)

Tony (*as* Enid *passes him*). Did you hear the one about the young woman from Fleet?
Enid (*firmly*). We did not—and we don't want to.

(*She walks quickly up stage and exits through the hall.*)

Tony (*looking at* Ann). What do you bet she'll ask me to tell her when we're alone? Aren't you coming, Ann? (*He moves to the* R. *end of the settee.*)
Ann. No—No, I think I'd rather not! I've got rather a headache. I'll stay here by the fire. (*She moves to the light switch up* R. *and turns out the main lights and returns to the fireplace.*)

Tony (*making a half move towards her*). It looks jolly attractive by that fire.

Ann (*sadly*). Does it, Ton-ey?

Tony. Yes, by jove, it does. (*He makes another half step towards her.*)

(Olivia *appears in the doorway* R. *She has thrown an opera cloak around her and makes a striking figure.*)

Olivia (*very firmly*). Coming, Tony?

Tony (*swinging round*). What? Oh, yes—yes, rather. Coming, Olivia.

(Tony *moves towards the archway and exits through the hall.* Olivia *smiles sweetly at* Ann *and exits through the hall, switching out the hall light as she goes.*)

Ann (*with vigour*). Beast!

(*She puts the small table back in its place down* L. *and sits in the armchair above the fireplace. She picks up the poker, stirs the fire, then sits thinking for a moment.* Alice *enters quietly from the hall.* Ann *throws the poker into the fireplace with a clatter.*)

Beast!

(Alice *screams.*)

(*She turns round and jumps up.*) Oh, Alice!

Alice (*moving into the room a few paces*). You frightened the life out of me. Whatever are you doing there all by yourself, miss?

Ann (*sitting in the armchair*). Just *being* all by myself.

Alice (*moving behind the settee*). Why didn't you go with the others, Miss Ann?

Ann. I wanted to be alone.

Alice. There's worse company.

Ann (*sadly*). But not much.

Alice. I suppose I'd better draw the curtains?

Ann. Not a bit like Christmas. No snow—all just hard and cruel (*very sadly*) like men's hearts.

Alice. For one so young, miss, you talk remarkable good sense. (*She draws the curtains.*)

Ann. You've been crossed in love, too, haven't you, Alice?

Alice. Crossed? (*She moves above the* L. *end of the settee.*) I've been more than crossed—I've been zig-zagged.

Ann. I'm beginning to feel that way myself.

Alice. What! Is it Miss Olivia and Mr Tony?

Ann. It is.

Alice. How blind men are. Miss Olivia's *outside* attracts them. It's her *inside* they won't like. Now, *your* inside . . .

Ann. Oh, dear, I wish I had a better outside, never mind about the other.

Alice. Nothing wrong with it, Miss Ann. Some man will see

that soon enough. As for Mr Tony, Miss Olivia's just dazzled him. She can be a thousand candle-power lamp when she wants to be. (*She moves towards the archway.*)

ANN. And I'm only a poor little fifty-watt.

ALICE (*turning*). Anything you want now, miss? A nice cup of tea?

ANN. No, thanks, really—I'm all right.

(ALICE *exits through the hall.* ANN *stirs the fire again. She puts the poker down, rises, and taking a magazine from the armchair down* L., *stands facing the fireplace, flicking over the pages. She throws it on the armchair down* L., *moves to the radiogram, and turns it on. The "Children's Overture" can be heard, very faintly. She returns to the fireplace and picks up the magazine. Through the music can be heard the faint sound of sleigh bells.* ANN *looks puzzled and sits in the armchair above the fireplace. After a moment or two she rises, moves to the radiogram and switches it off. She listens for a moment, facing down* L. *The window curtains silently open, unaided.* ANN *slowly turns to the window. Then the windows undo themselves and begin to open.* ANN *gives a gasp. The figure of a man is disclosed. He is dressed in rather suggestively burglarious clothes, a check cap and an old suit, perhaps. He is not by any means a young man, indeed he looks well over sixty, possibly over seventy. His face is wrinkled and lined, but is full of quite extraordinary vitality. He has grey hair, rather untidily arranged. His voice is Cockney, with occasional lapses into something quite different. His movements are quiet and active. See the Note at the end of the Play.*)

ANN. Ooh! Whatever are you doing there. Have you broken in?

NICHOLAS (*agreeably and quietly*). Oh, no, miss. Not *broken*. Everything's intact. (*There's a slight suggestion of an "h" before the word.*) Very careful to break nothing, I was.

ANN. But you—you're a burg-lar.

NICHOLAS. Well (*entering a few paces into the room*) I'd say that's putting it a bit strong, you know. Couldn't we find a better word?

(*The windows close.*)

Ann. Good gracious! I shall have to send for the police.

NICHOLAS (*slightly towards her*). Just a moment! Just a moment. Is that fair? Is that right? I asks you.

ANN. But you deserve . . .

NICHOLAS. Bless you. I'm not worrying about myself, lady. But think of the poor police. Christmas Eve. Poor old "sarge" just stuffing his young Freddie's Christmas stocking full of good things for tomorrow. And you ring him up and drag him from the job. Bless you—it ain't considerate, it ain't Christian, is it now?

ANN. You really *are* an extraordinary burglar. And, how on earth did you know that our sergeant *had* a little boy called Freddie?

NICHOLAS. Why, Lord love you. The police and I haven't got no secrets from each other.

ANN (*returning to look at him*). And, surely, you're rather—ra-ther *old* to be a burglar?

NICHOLAS (*a little sadly*). You've said it, lady. I should have retired from my job. But, you see, not exactly being a civil servant, a grateful country don't give me no pension.

ANN. But how terrible. Would you—would you like something to eat?

NICHOLAS. Well—not to *eat*—but—if you *was* to ask me . . .

ANN. Something to drink?

NICHOLAS. Now, that *is* an idea.

ANN (*moving to the table up* R.). Lemonade?

NICHOLAS. Good idea.

ANN. Or beer?

NICHOLAS. Better idea.

ANN. Or whisky?

NICHOLAS. Best idea.

ANN (*pouring out the drink*). I don't think this can be quite right of me.

NICHOLAS. Well, I wouldn't say that. (*He moves below the* L. *end of the settee.*) Nothing so very wrong with it. Here we are, you and I, just two social outcasts.

ANN (*moving down stage below the* R. *end of the settee*). What *do* you mean? (*She hands him a drink.*)

NICHOLAS (*taking the drink*). Well, it's simple, ain't it? If there hadn't been *something* wrong you would've been off with the others.

ANN. With the others? You mean, you watched them go?

NICHOLAS. Of course I did. Well. (*He looks at her and raises his glass.*) Happy Christmas. Look here, miss, I feel all lonesome—drinking this on my own. Won't you have something yourself?

ANN. Well, I don't know, really.

NICHOLAS (*putting his glass on the table below the settee*). Course you will. Now, what'll it be? (*He moves to the table up* R.) Shall I read *your* thoughts for you? I'll tell you what you'd like.

ANN. Well then, guess.

NICHOLAS (*pouring out the drink*). Not guessing—thought-reading.

ANN (*moving towards the fireplace*). I'll bet you can't really read thoughts.

NICHOLAS. O.K., lady. I'll take you on. A real bet. But no—you daren't.

ANN. Of course I dare. What's the bet?

NICHOLAS (*thinking for a moment*). Not so easy, that. You see, if we made it money I couldn't pay you. Tell you what. If you win I'll promise you on my solemn word never to do any housebreaking again.

ANN. Yes?

c

NICHOLAS (*slowly*). And if I win (*he pauses*) there's a chauffeur's room over the garage with no-one in it. If I win, you'll let me sleep the night there and not tell anyone?

ANN. All right then, I will. (*She sits in the armchair above the fireplace.*)

NICHOLAS (*dispensing the drinks*). It's a bet! Well, here's my thought-reading. (*He looks at the glass.*) About an inch of orange, about half an inch of gin, fill up with soda, and add just *two* drops of peach bitters.

ANN. But, that's *marvellous*! How *did* you know?

NICHOLAS (*crossing to the fireplace he hands* ANN *the drink and sits in the armchair down* L.). Ah! (*He nods his head in a mysterious fashion.*) So I've won?

ANN. You've won. What's your name?

NICHOLAS. Mr Nicholas.

ANN. Mr Nicholas? That's a very Christmassy name.

NICHOLAS. I'm a very Christmassy person.

ANN. It seems funny our sitting here like this. Whatever will you do if Alice comes in?

NICHOLAS. She won't. And if she did, you'll just tell her it's your old friend Mr Nicholas just back from winter sports at Saintey Mauritzey.

ANN. Switzerland? I haven't been there yet! Oh, dear, I wish our weather were a bit more like Switzerland.

NICHOLAS. You're partial to a bit of snow?

ANN. Well, it doesn't seem like Christmas without it.

NICHOLAS. No, it don't, do it? Which reminds me—we'd better draw those curtains. (*He rises and moves to the windows.*)

ANN. Yes, it would be safer. (*She drinks her cocktail.*)

(NICHOLAS *makes a gesture at the curtains. They close.*)

Mr Nicholas, can you really read thoughts?

NICHOLAS (*turning to her*). Quite often.

ANN. Read mine.

NICHOLAS (*returning to the fireplace*). Okey-Doke! (*He stands looking at her for a moment, then sits beside her on the* R. *arm of the chair.*) You're thinking of . . .

ANN. Yes?

NICHOLAS. A young man.

ANN. Go on.

NICHOLAS. Nice young man. Bit impressionable. He's fallen for your sister.

ANN (*in astonishment*). Mr Nich-o-las!

NICHOLAS. Very simple. Saw him go out with her, looking all goopey-like.

ANN. It's marvellous.

NICHOLAS. Nothing marvellous about it. When a young lady

has a look in her eye like you have, she's thinking of a young man.
(*Slowly.*) You know, miss . . .

ANN. Well?

NICHOLAS. We all have our moments.

ANN. Moments?

NICHOLAS (*careful of the way he speaks, slowly*). Those moments
in your life which nothing, nothing, will ever make you forget.
Perhaps that funny lonely feeling you have at the seaside in the
evening, when you're going off to bed, and the sea is rolling up to
you, asking you to stay and play with it a little longer—when you
watch a pebble dropping into a perfectly clear little moorland
pool—dropping slowly, slowly to the bottom—or a dragon-fly,
perched on a leaf of laurel, looking at you through its green glass
eyes . . .

ANN (*whispering*). Yes—go on—go on.

NICHOLAS. And when you're older, the melody of a half-
remembered song—a bundle of letters, tied up with ribbon—
the scent of a wayside blossom, as you walk along a leafy lane—
or, maybe, a child's eyes—(*he pauses*) that remind you of someone else's—Those are Moments.

(*There is silence for a moment.*)

ANN. Mr Nicholas, you have the most wond-erful voice.

NICHOLAS (*lapsing into Cockney*). My mother made me have
lessons in elocution, she did. And now, shall I tell you what you'd
like best for a Christmas present?

·(*The sound of children's voices singing a Christmas carol is heard.*)

ANN. Oh, do—*do*.

NICHOLAS. You'd like your young man back again.

ANN. If I only could. Do you hear the children singing carols,
Mr Nicholas?

NICHOLAS. Very nice, too.

ANN. Do you think I could ever get my—my young man back
again?

NICHOLAS. If that sister of yours fell for someone else—you
might.

ANN. But there isn't anyone else at present she *would* fall for.

NICHOLAS. Now that *is* a pity—a real pity. (*He thinks for a
moment.*) I'd be a proper magician if I could find that someone
else, wouldn't I?

ANN. You would, indeed.

(NICHOLAS *yawns and stretches his arms. He makes a commanding gesture
towards the telephone on the writing table. It instantly rings.*)

NICHOLAS. What a shame I can't . . .

(*The telephone rings.*)

Better answer that.

ANN (*rising, moving to the writing table and picking up the receiver*). Who is that? Sorry, I can't catch the name. (*To* NICHOLAS.) It's a long-distance call.

NICHOLAS. Long-distance? Perhaps it's from Fairyland?

(*The children's voices grow fainter.*)

ANN. Yes—yes, who is it? . . . Mr Linsitt. What? Not you, George? Good gracious, we thought you were in Canada . . . You've just landed? . . . Of course—of course—Yes, *of course* we can put you up. When can you get here? . . . Good! . . . Olivia? Oh, yes, *rather*, she'll be just thrilled to death . . . You are? Well, so is she—positively longing to see you—I'll tell her. I'll tell her *immediately* . . . Yes, come along at once. (*She puts down the receiver.*) Mr Nicholas, you *are* a magician.

(*The children's voices grow louder.*)

NICHOLAS. Why?

ANN (*moving above the settee to* R. *of* NICHOLAS). That was from George Linsitt—the only man for whom Olivia, my sister, *really fell*. And he went back to Canada and now he's coming *here*. *Coming here*. Isn't it wond-erful? (*She sits in the armchair above the fireplace.*) It's just too marvellous. Exactly when you were speaking about it.

NICHOLAS. My Christmas present to you.

ANN. What a *wonderful* Christmas it's going to be. Only one thing wanting.

(NICHOLAS *stands up. The voices are now very loud.*)

NICHOLAS. What?

ANN. Snow.

(NICHOLAS *moves to the french windows.*)

NICHOLAS (*with his back to her*). You're hoping for a white Christmas, aren't you?

ANN (*facing front*). That's too much to hope for.

NICHOLAS. Nothing's too much to hope for—at Christmas.

(ANN *turns to him. He moves to the extreme* R. *of the windows and makes another commanding gesture and the curtains open. The trees are now quite white—covered with snow—and snow is falling lightly, but regularly.* ANN *rises. The voices ring out very loudly.* ANN *moves to the windows.*)

ANN (*slowly, and with a gasp as she looks at the scene outside*). Oh, Mist-er Nich-o-las!

(*The windows open and* ANN *moves through them and stands for a few moments in the falling snow, her arms stretched up in ecstasy.*)

Mister Nicholas!

The CURTAIN *falls.*

ACT II

Scene.—*The same. About half-past three on the afternoon of Christmas Day.*

Before the Curtain *rises the music of "Shepherd's Hey" is heard, and as it rises, we hear that it comes from the direction of the radiogram.*

Alice *is dusting things—for no other reason really—rather viciously. She is at the writing table when* Uncle Ned *enters. He is obviously in the best of spirits.*

Alice (*bending over the writing table*). This *has* been dusted. So has this.

Ned (*approaching* Alice; *humming the tune*). Te-*tum*-tum-tum, te-*tum*, tum-tum. Tum-te-te-te tum-te-te-te tum-tum-TUM! (*On the last "Tum" he smacks her gently and moves quickly behind the settee.*)

(Alice *turns round with a wrathful cry.* Ned, *however, is sailing away from her now with an expression of innocence upon his face.*)

Te-*tum*-tum-tum. . . .

Alice. Mr Edward! You surprise me.

Ned (*with a leer; moving towards her*). I surprise myself sometimes.

Alice (*moving to the table below the settee; tartly*). Gentlemen of your age often surprise themselves. (*She bends over the table.*)

(Ned *veers in her direction, and is about to administer another smack when* Alice *abruptly turns round.*)

Ned (*veering away again to up* r.). Te-*tum*-tum-tum. (*He feels in his pocket and produces some notes.*)

Alice. Look here, Mr Edward . . .

Ned (*holding up the notes and moving behind and below the* l. *end of the settee*). Look *here!* With best wishes for a Happy Christmas. (*He hands some notes to* Alice.)

Alice. For me, sir? (*She smiles.*) Oh, sir—sir.

Ned (*hastily*). Yes. I know I'm breaking the rule—no Christmas presents till six o'clock—but I want you to do something for me. All I want is (*he whispers*) an extra blanket on my bed.

Alice. A what?

Ned (*moving to the fireplace; getting a little annoyed*). Turn off that cursed wireless!

(Alice *moves quickly to the radiogram and switches it off.*)

An extra blanket on my bed.

ALICE. My goodness! Another? You'll be stifled. (*She pronounces it "stiffled".*)

NED (*angrily*). Whether I'm "stiffled" or not is my own affair, isn't it? (*He rubs his lip.*) I'm getting shingles on my lips. This house is as cold as a refrigerator. I've never been here without getting a chill. And the unexpected fall of snow.

(ANN *comes down the stairs and enters the room a few paces.* NED *turns to* ANN *and smiles the moment he sees her.*)

ALICE. If you insist, Mr Edward.
NED. I do!

(ALICE *exits through the hall, shaking her head.*)

ANN (*moving to* NED *and handing him a lipstick*). Mummy told me to give you this. She forgot to give it to you before. (*She moves below the* L. *end of the settee.*)

NED (*takes it with interest*). What do I do with it—eh? Rub it on? (*He does so and glances at himself in the mirror, over the fireplace.*) Your mother's right. It doesn't show. (*He puts out his tongue and licks his lips.*) Tastes like sweet shrimps. (*Suddenly.*) Ann, who's this new youngster, George what's-his-name? Where did he come from—eh? What's he after—eh?

ANN. He's been working in Canada. (*She sits at the* L. *end of the settee.*) Used to be a great friend of Olivia's.

NED. That so? That so, indeed? Well, (*he drops his voice to a whisper*) don't believe a word of it. Wouldn't trust him an inch.

ANN. But, why?

NED (*darkly*). Something funny about the fellow. He laughs too much—laughs too quickly—laughs at *me*. Am I anything to laugh at?

ANN. No, Uncle Ned. (*She looks towards the archway.*)

NED. Then, why is he always bursting with laughter when he sees me. Damned little whipper-snapper.

ANN (*seeing* GEORGE *about to enter from the hall*). S-sh!

(GEORGE LINSITT *enters from the hall. He is about twenty-five, a pleasant-looking, rather ingenuous youth, with a permanent smile, and a ready laugh. He is inclined to carry candour rather too far, but he is blissfully unaware of it. He moves a few paces into the room.*)

NED (*crossing above the settee towards* GEORGE; *with awful heartiness*). Hello, George, my boy. (*He attempts an appalling trans-oceanic accent.*) How's things? You sure are looking fine. So what?

GEORGE (*immediately laughing heartily*). Gosh! Uncle Ned. If I don't find you the biggest laugh yet.

NED (*angrily*). You do, do you? Thank you. I'm much obliged. (*His voice takes on an angry snarl.*) Funny old gentleman? Ha! Ha! Real old comic. Eh?

GEORGE (*delighted*). You've said it, Uncle Ned. You've said it.

NED. And what, may I ask, do you find so comic about me?

GEORGE (*completely unembarrassed*). Aw—it's hard to put that into words.

ANN (*hastily*). I wouldn't try, George. I *really* wouldn't try.

NED (*stiffly*). Thank you, Ann. But I should like to hear what this young man has to say about me.

GEORGE (*unwarily*). Well—well—you see, sir, in Canada, in the comic strips, there's always a dear old gentleman representing the typical Britisher. You know—(*he gesticulates as he speaks*) nice, white-grey hair—sweet, ruddy complexion—*lovely* little Mary covered with a Union Jack.

NED. Go on.

GEORGE (*surveying him, with his head on one side, as though to get the picture*). Why, you're him, down to the bottom button.

NED. Well, I'm flattered! (*With growing wrath.*) I'm flattered at being taken for a Britisher.

ANN (*seeking appeasement*). So you and George do agree, after all?

NED (*not to be put off his row*). We do *not*! (*He moves* L. *of the settee.*) And I'd have you remember, George finds me a ridiculous figure.

GEORGE (*moving to the* R. *of the settee*). Hold hard there, Uncle Ned. Not ridiculous. I'll guess not. I never said ridiculous. I never said I found you that. No, sir!

NED. Then perhaps you'll tell me just what you *do* find me?

GEORGE (*quite simply*). Why, sir, I find you a fine old English gentleman.

NED (*very agreeably surprised*). Indeed? Well 'pon my word, I expected something quite different. (*He moves to the fireplace and faces them.*) That's not too bad—not too bad at all. A fine old English gentleman. (*He laughs delightedly.*)

GEORGE (*joining in the laugh with zest*). And one grand rip-roaring belly-ache of a laugh.

NED. *What!*

ANN (*rising and moving quickly to* NED). Uncle Ned!—Uncle Ned! —Quick, you've forgotten.

NED. Forgotten what?

ANN. Don't you always ring up your old friend, Mr Sant, at half-past three on Christmas Day? It's just that now.

NED. So it is! I wouldn't miss it for a fortune. I'll phone from the Hall. Every Christmas Day for the last eighteen years.

(GEORGE laughs.)

So that's funny, too, is it? Well, (*he moves to* GEORGE *and claps him on the back*) I'll tell you something that'll *really* make you laugh. Did you hear the name of the friend I'm ringing up? Sant—Sant— And his Christian name is—is—*Charley*. (*He pauses for* GEORGE *to laugh.*) You see it? Charley Sant—Charley's Aunt . . .

(*He explodes with laughter and exits through the hall.* GEORGE, *however, is quite unmoved and stands looking after him in astonishment.*)

GEORGE (*slowly, and in a puzzled voice*). Now, what the heck's funny in that?

ANN. Nothing, really, especially if you've heard it almost every Christmas Day since you've been born. (*She hesitates.*) Enjoying yourself, George?

GEORGE (*hesitating*). Aw—Ann—it's just perfect being here—but . . .

ANN. But what, George?

GEORGE. Well, (*moving behind and to the* L. *of the settee*) it seems sort of queer telling *you* this, Ann, but I'm disappointed.

ANN. Disappointed?

GEORGE. You see, Ann—Olivia (*sitting on the* L. *arm of the settee*) she seems sort of different. Maybe it's my fault—maybe I've been away too long. But she's all caught up with this Tony fellow. She don't seem to have no time for me. I—I'd like your advice, Ann.

ANN. My advice? (*She moves to him.*) I don't think I could give you advice. (*She thinks.*) Or, could I?

GEORGE. If you'd tell me what I'm doing wrong. I thought your sister and me were good friends—that's why I've come back from Canada. But (*in a dejected voice*) maybe, maybe I've made a mistake.

ANN. Oh, no, George. (*She moves behind the settee to* R.C.) I—I'm sure she's very fond of you still. But, George . . .

GEORGE (*without looking at her*). Yeah?

ANN. Perhaps you aren't tack-ling her *quite* the right way.

GEORGE (*looking at her*). You mean . . . ?

ANN (*moving below the* R. *end of the settee*). Per-haps you're letting her see a bit too (*sitting on the settee*) too clearly that you're in love with her.

GEORGE (*turning on the arm of the settee*). Well! Doesn't she *want* to see it?

ANN (*hastily*). I don't know—but I wondered.

GEORGE. Wondered what?

ANN. If you pretended—just pretended—you weren't quite so keen on her. If you pretended you were keen on—on someone else . . .

GEORGE. I see what you mean. And I reckon (*he pauses to think*) I reckon you're dead right. But (*crestfallen*) who else could I pretend to be keen on?

ANN. Don't you know any other girls in England?

GEORGE. No-one—except you, of course.

ANN (*rising; full of fire*). Well, there is—there is me.

GEORGE (*rising, as though making a discovery*). Gosh! So there is! (*Promptly.*) Can I pretend to be in love with you?

ANN (*equally promptly*). Certainly, you can.

George. Gee! (*He moves close to her.*) Nothing like beginning well, is there? (*He draws her to him and kisses her.*)

Ann (*horrified*). Oh, George! George! You mustn't do that. At least—at least—only when Olivia's looking.

George. What's the harm when we're only pretending?

(*He draws her to him again and is beginning to kiss her as* Tony *enters from the hall.*)

Tony (*moving a few paces into the room; astonished*). Great Heavens!

George (*with a smile*). Anything troubling you, buddy?

Tony (*not too happily*). Oh, nothing. Nothing at all. Nice to see you making yourself comfortable.

George. Thanks. I like it, too.

Tony. I must say you Colonials don't lose any time making yourselves at home. (*He moves between the chair and the* R. *end of the settee.*)

George (*moving a step below* Ann; *to* Tony). I'll tell you something you don't know, too. We Colonials don't like being called Colonials.

Tony. That's just too bad, isn't it?

George (*moving to the* L. *of* Tony). Not so bad it can't be corrected.

Tony. Just what do you mean by that?

George. Just what I say.

Ann (*hastily moving between them*). Oh, boys—you mustn't quarrel about me.

George (*with awful candour*). Gosh, Ann! We were quarrelling about a word, not about you.

(Ann *moves above* George *to the fireplace.*)

Ann (*disappointed*). Is that all?

(George *follows her and stops above the* L. *end of the settee.*)

Tony. Your mother wants those fairy lights for the table to-night. D'you know where they are?

Ann (*without turning*). Yes. They're in the chauffeur's room over the garage. (*She suddenly checks herself and swings round.*) No—no—they're *not* there.

Tony. Of course they are. (*He is about to make a move up* R.) I remember now, I saw them there.

Ann (*taking a step* R.). No, Tony, *really*.

Tony. What on earth's the matter, Ann?

(Olivia *enters from the hall.* George *immediately moves to the* R. *of* Ann.)

Olivia (*moving* L. *of* Tony). Hello, George.

George (*cursorily*). Hello. (*To* Ann; *in a different voice.*) Ann, darling, you promised you'd take me for a walk. (*He slips his arm round her waist.*) I'm dying to see the village green, the duck pond, and the oldest inhabitants.

ANN (*alarmed*). But I didn't—there isn't a village green, *or a* duck pond, and the inhabitants are all very young.

OLIVIA (*moving above the* R. *end of the settee*). Of course they are. George, if you aren't doing anything, I've a nice little job for you. Would you like to help me to hang up the holly?

GEORGE (*not looking at* OLIVIA). Sorry. I've got a date.

OLIVIA. *And* the mistletoe?

GEORGE. My date's with the mistletoe, thanks. (*He smiles at* ANN.)

OLIVIA. Of course—if you'd rather . . .

GEORGE (*cheerfully*). Sure, I would, if you'll pardon me.

OLIVIA (*angrily*). Really! Tony, what about those electric things?

TONY (*watching* GEORGE *and* ANN). Oh, they're in the duck pond.

OLIVIA (*swinging round to* TONY). What!

TONY. I mean—in the chauffeur's room.

OLIVIA. I'll help you get them.

(OLIVIA *exits through the hall.*)

TONY (*meaningly*). Congratulations, Ann. Hot work. Damn hot, hot work. (*He looks rather displeased.*)

(TONY *exits through the hall.*)

ANN. Oh dear, George. You *do* work quickly, don't you?

GEORGE (*with ferocious energy*). I *love* this work.

ANN. Good gracious! (*She crosses in front of* GEORGE *towards the hall.*) I must stop Tony going to the chauffeur's room.

GEORGE (*moving round the back of the settee to intercept* ANN *at* R.C.). What's wrong with the chauffeur's room, anyway? Just suit old Tony, I'd say.

ANN (*suddenly turning on him*). You mustn't say anything horrid about Tony.

GEORGE (*with a broad grin*). So *that's* how the land lies? Gee, but I do say you're smart.

ANN. What do you mean?

GEORGE. Sort of Mutual Benefit Society, this. You put the heat on Tony while I hot up Olivia. That was the idea, wasn't it?

ANN. No!

GEORGE (*insistingly*). Yes?

ANN (*giving in*). Yes.

GEORGE. Great! You've got a lot of brains in that little head of yours.

ANN. Oh, no, George. I'm not in the least bit clever.

GEORGE. I'd say you are. Sister Olivia may have the looks, but . . .

ANN. George! (*She moves* R. *of the chair.*)

GEORGE. Oh, gee! (*He moves above the* L. *end of the settee.*) That's not what I meant to say at all. (*He is hopelessly confused.*) I mean—Olivia's all flashy, you know, but you're pretty, too—in a homely way . . .

ANN (*tragically*). A homely way?

GEORGE (*desperately*). The sort of person you'd like to share a home with. (*He sighs in relief at getting that off his chest.*)

ANN. That's a *little* better—but not very much.

GEORGE (*moving below the* L. *end of the settee*). Oh, for Pete's sake, don't mind what I say. (*He sits at the* L. *end of the settee.*) I'm a complete fool at trying to express myself. You see, Ann, I've had a lonely sort of life for the last couple of years.

ANN (*moving to the front of the settee*). Poor George! (*She sits on the settee.*)

GEORGE. Out there in the country, with hardly a soul to speak to—I've been—well—I've been sex-starved. (*He puts his arm round* ANN.)

ANN (*startled*). What! (*She edges a little away from* GEORGE.) I hope you're not hungry now, George.

GEORGE. All the time out there I've been thinking of Olivia—Olivia all the time—and it sort of gets on one's brain.

ANN. What does?

GEORGE. Olivia.

ANN. I wish I got on someone's brain.

GEORGE. I'm not going to answer that one; for, if I do, I reckon I'd say the wrong thing. But, what I do say, Ann . . .

(MARY *enters from the hall. She is looking a little worried.*)

MARY (*moving to the* R. *of* ANN). Ann, have you any idea what can be going on between your uncle and Alice? They seem to be having a free fight—in his bedroom.

ANN. Perhaps Uncle Ned's sex-starved, too.

MARY. What!

ANN (*confused*). Oh! It's all right. He—he just wants an extra blanket.

MARY (*moving to* R.C.). I see. Well, George, are they looking after you properly?

GEORGE (*rising*). Gosh, Mrs Meldon. It's *me* that should be doing the looking after. May I go up and see Mr Meldon some time?

MARY. Yes, do. Go before tea, if you don't mind.

GEORGE. Tough luck on him being out of all this Christmas fun.

MARY (*thoughtfully*). All this Christmas fun? Yes, I suppose it is! All the same, he's managed to miss quite a lot of trouble.

GEORGE. Trouble?

Mary. Christmas comes but once a year. If it came twice it would really be unbearable.

(Topsey *bursts into the room from the hall. She is excited and angry.*)

Topsey (*moving down to the* r. *of* Mary). There's a man in the house.

Mary. Good Heavens! Where?

Topsey. Running down the steps from that chauffeur's room of yours.

Mary. Gracious! What was he like?

Topsey. A complete scoundrel, if ever I set eyes on one.

Mary. Ann, who on earth can it be?

Ann. Who on earth . . . ?

Mary (*to* Topsey). What did you do?

Topsey. I screamed.

George (*admiringly*). I'll bet you did.

Topsey. You weren't asked!

(George *subsides.*)

Fortunately, Tony saw him and ran after him. I hope he catches the blackguard.

Ann (*rising*). I hope he doesn't.

Topsey (*quickly*). What d'you mean by that?

(Ann *moves towards the french windows.*)

Man's certainly a burglar—probably a murderer. Good Heavens! He might have got into *my* bedroom.

George (*smiling*). Gee! And I reckon only one of you would have come out alive.

Ann (*at the french windows*). Oh! Good gracious me.

Topsey (*moving to the* r. *of* Ann). Ah! So Tony's got him. Good! He'll spend his Christmas evening in the lock-up. (*She opens the french windows and calls out loudly.*) Bring him in! Bring him in! Bring the scoundrel in.

George (*moving to* Mary). You know, I always heard the English country was supposed to be dull, but gee—it's fun and games all the time here.

Ann (*turning to* George). Fun and games?

(Mr Nicholas *enters through the french windows followed and held by* Tony, *who wears an overcoat and muffler. The grip on* Mr Nicholas *is gentle but firm.* Ann *closes the windows.*)

Topsey (*backing behind the settee*). That's he! That's the ruffian.

(George *moves down* r. Ann *moves behind the armchair above the fireplace.* Mr Nicholas *stands for a moment as though abashed.* Tony *releases his hold.*)

Nicholas (*moving between the armchair and the settee*). Happy Christmas, all.

Topsey (*furiously*). Of all the impertinence.

Nicholas. No, ma'am—not an impertinence to wish you a *happy* Christmas. Now, if I'd wished you an unhappy . . .

Topsey. Be quiet! Who are you?

Nicholas. Name of Nicholas, ma'am.

(Tony *moves above the* l. *end of the settee.*)

Mary. What were you doing in our garage?

Nicholas. Ah! That's a long story—and a sad story. But, there—I can't expect you to understand. It ain't easy to be *really* sorry for strangers' troubles, is it, ma'am?

Tony. As a matter of fact, what *were* you doing?

Nicholas. Since you press the question, sir, I took the liberty of passing the night in that little room above the garage. No harm meant.

Topsey. No harm? Indeed!

Nicholas. No harm, indeed, ma'am. And it was that or the workhouse. Now *you* wouldn't like to have spent Christmas Day in the workhouse? The paupers say such horribly rude things about the Christmas pudding.

(Topsey, *disgusted, turns up stage,* r. *of the Christmas tree.*)

George (*with a yell of laughter*). Gosh! Isn't he great?

Tony (*moving above the* r. *end of the settee, laughing*). You'll have to let him go after that, Mrs Meldon.

Ann. There's nothing so terribly wrong in—in Mr Nicholas spending the night in the chauffeur's room.

Topsey (*moving down* r. *of* Mary). A lot of silver there'd have been left if you hadn't caught him. I expect half of it's gone already.

Ann. Nonsense, Aunt Topsey. (*She moves round the standard lamp to the front of the fireplace.*)

Topsey (*to* Mary). You'd better send for the police.

Nicholas (*to* Topsey). You couldn't do it, ma'am. Your kind heart wouldn't let you.

George (*sitting in the chair*). Not exactly the Christmas spirit, is it?

Topsey. What's Christmas got to do with it?

Mary. Well, I really don't want to. I don't see any reason why . . .

(Ned *enters from the hall.*)

Ned. Ann—that damn line's engaged. (*Suddenly his eyes light on* Nicholas.) I beg your pardon. (*He moves to* Nicholas.) How do you do, sir? (*He shakes* Nicholas *by the hand.*) Happy Christmas! (*He looks at* Nicholas.) Surely we have met before?

Nicholas (*sadly*). I'm sure we have, sir!

Mary. Ned, Tony found this man running out of the chauffeur's room. Apparently he spent the night there.

Topsey. A burglar. You've only to look at him.

Ned (*judicially*). What! What do I hear? A burglar? Breaking into the house? This is serious (*scowling at* Nicholas) very serious indeed.

Topsey. The police—it's their business.

Ned (*severely, to* Topsey). Kindly leave this matter to me. You forget I am a Justice of the Peace.

Nicholas. Lumme! I said we'd met before.

Tony. Well, I don't think there's anything to be done. He hasn't pinched anything—or, have you?

Ann. Of course, he hasn't. (*She sits in the armchair down* l.)

Topsey ⎫
George ⎬ (*together*). ⎰ What do you know about it?
Mary ⎭ ⎱ Give him a break!
⎱ I wish, Ned, that you'd . . .

Ned (*in his most judicial fashion*). Mary. Do you wish to leave this affair in my hands?

Mary. Of course. You'll know what to do so much better than I.

Ned. In that case, I wish to question this man.

Topsey. Let the police do that.

Ned (*severely*). And I wish to question him alone. (*He looks at* Topsey.) Alone, I said.

Mary (*hastily*). It would be very good of you if you would. Come along, Topsey. Come along, all of you.

(Mary *takes hold of* Topsey's *arm and leads her to the archway.*)

Topsey (*as she moves*). The man's a criminal. He'll only make a fool of you.

Ned (*severely*). That is, possibly, not as simple as you think. And he *must* be heard. (*Striking an attitude.*) "Fiat justitia, ruat caelum!"

(Topsey *and* Mary *exit through the hall.* Tony *tries to attract* Ann's *attention.* Ann *ignores him.*)

George (*rising and moving between the chair and the settee*). Gosh! Isn't he a wow?

Ned (*angrily*). Are you suggesting that I—*I*—am a—wow?

Ann (*rising and hastily crossing to* George). Come along, George, we'll have a game of billiards. (*She ushers* George *towards the archway.*)

Tony. Mind if I join in?

Ann (*over her shoulder*). Don't worry, Ton-ey. We're all right as we are, aren't we, George?

George. Sure.

(Ann *and* George *exit through the hall.*)

Tony. Well, I'm . . .

(Tony *strides across to the door* r. *and exits.*)

Ned (*taking out his watch, looking at it and moving* r. *of the settee*).

Now, my man—*now*, my man. (*Fiercely.*) What were you doing sleeping in the chauffeur's room?

Nicholas (*moving down a little*). Sleeping, sir.

Ned (*warming up*). I warn you, I'm not to be trifled with. Dammit, man, haven't you got a home?

Nicholas. I've been in a lot of homes, sir. But you wouldn't call them home.

Ned. That's bad. That's bad. What's your trade?—You must have one.

Nicholas. Well, sir, I do a bit of all sorts. Toy making . . .

Ned. Toy making?

Nicholas. Yes. I work for most of the year at that. Then, round Christmas, I do a lot of driving.

Ned. Driving what?

Nicholas. Almost everything. But I prefer a sleigh.

Ned. A sleigh? Are you pulling my leg—eh?

Nicholas. Oh no, sir! You see, I spent a lot of my time in Norway. And then, I do a bit of magic.

Ned (*feeling in his pocket for his tobacco pouch*). What do you mean by magic?

Nicholas. Well, it goes with the rest of the work in a sort of a way.

Ned (*still feeling in his pocket; indicating to* Nicholas *to sit on the settee*). Do you mean conjuring?

Nicholas (*sitting at the* L. *end of the settee*). A little less and a little more than that, sir! Illusion, you know—making things vanish.

Ned. Used to be a bit of a magician myself. Still know a few tricks. Quite a dab at it once. (*Suddenly.*) Where the blazes is my tobacco pouch? I've lost it!

Nicholas. No, you haven't, sir.

Ned. What do you mean—eh?

Nicholas. Left jacket pocket, sir.

(Ned *feels in his left pocket and brings out the pouch.*)

Ned. How the devil did you know that? Magic—eh?

Nicholas. No, sir. Only pocket you didn't look in.

Ned. Very smart. Very observant.

Nicholas. Always smoke *Three Triangles*, sir?

Ned. How did you know that?

Nicholas (*inadvertently taking out his pipe*). Thought-reading, I suppose. Sort of comes to me.

Ned. Good! Have a fill. (*He hands the pouch to* Nicholas.)

Nicholas. Thank you, sir. (*He fills his pipe, rises and places the tobacco pouch on the table below the settee.*)

Ned (*testily*). Sit down, man, sit down. What the devil are you standing for?

(Nicholas *sits.*)

So you're a conjuror—eh ? I'll show *you* something

that'll surprise you. (*He looks round in the direction of the writing table.*) Pack of cards, that's what I want.

NICHOLAS. One here, sir. (*He takes a pack of playing cards from the table in front of the settee and passes it to* NED.)

NED (*taking the cards*). Good! (*He moves behind the settee to the standard lamp.*) Let's have a bit of light to help us. (*He switches on the standard lamp and places it* R. *of the armchair above the fireplace.*) All done in full light and above board . . . eh? (*He stands by* NICHOLAS *and shuffles the cards as he is speaking, taking a surreptitious peep at one now and then.*) Patience pack. Two of everything. Think that worries us? Not a bit. Not a bit.

NICHOLAS. Can see you've been a master at this game, sir.

NED (*modestly*). Only an amateur. Now. Choose a card. (*He spreads the cards out in his hands in front of* NICHOLAS. *It is perfectly obvious that he is trying to force one on him.*) Any one you like. Free choice, sir. Free choice.

(NICHOLAS *takes, or nearly takes, one which* NED *does not intend him to have.*)

Damn it! Any one you like. (*He forces the desired card on* NICHOLAS.)

(NICHOLAS *takes the card.*)

Now, look at it. Remember what it is, but don't tell me.

(NICHOLAS *looks at the card.*)

Now, put it back in the pack.

(NICHOLAS *puts the card back into the pack.*)

(*He immediately puts the little finger of his left hand into the pack above the card, to keep it separate. Then he half turns away from* NICHOLAS, *and, with a movement of cutting, brings the required card to the top.*) Good! Now we shuffle them. (*He shuffles them light-heartedly.*) And now *you* shuffle them. (*He hands the cards to* NICHOLAS *rather clumsily, as he has one concealed in his right palm.*) As many times as you like. And I won't look.

(NICHOLAS *shuffles the cards.*)

(*He turns away from* NICHOLAS, *and, whilst* NICHOLAS *is shuffling, has another surreptitious look at the card in his palm.*) Right? (*He turns round again.*) Give them to me.

(NICHOLAS *gives* NED *the cards.*)

And now! (*He suddenly counts out the cards on to the table in front of the settee.*) One, two, three, four (*with an air of triumph*) and five. Look at that card, sir. Take it up. Look at it. Is it yours?

(NICHOLAS *picks up the card, looks at it and puts it down.*)

It is?

(NICHOLAS *nods*.)

And, don't tell me—your card is the Knave of Diamonds. Right?

(NICHOLAS *nods stupified agreement*.)

Pretty hot—eh?

NICHOLAS. Blooming well boiling. And (*he takes up the tobacco pouch on the table*) the other Knave of Diamonds is in your tobacco pouch.

NED. What d'you mean?

(NICHOLAS *hands the pouch to* NED *who looks inside and draws out a Knave of Diamonds.* NED *is completely astonished*.)

Well, I'm—'pon my soul, I really am. How the—how the devil did you do that? Of course, I know. (*He looks a little guilty as he speaks.*) Of course, I know how you did it. What else can you do? (*He puts the pack of cards on the table below the settee and the pouch in his pocket.*)

(NICHOLAS *puts his pipe in his pocket, rises, moves to the fireplace, takes a box of matches from the mantelpiece, strikes a match and holds it up*.)

NICHOLAS. Blow that out.

NED (*moving a little nearer to* NICHOLAS). That's easy. (*He blows the match out.*)

NICHOLAS. This ain't quite so easy. (*He fills his lungs, takes an immense breath and blows violently at the standard lamp, which immediately goes out.*)

NED (*recoiling*). Good Heavens! (*He recovers himself.*) Do it again.

NICHOLAS (*puffing*). Bit hard on the respiratory system, sir.

NED (*eagerly*). Have a shot. (*He moves to the standard lamp, presses the switch once, then again, and the light comes on.*)

(NICHOLAS, *who is standing sideways to it, blows gently towards it out of the corner of his mouth. The light flickers. He glances at it with an annoyed expression on his face, blows a little harder, and the light goes out.*)

NED (*absolutely delighted*). Terrific! (*Eagerly.*) That *has* puzzled me.

(ANN *enters from the hall, a few paces into the room, and stands watching in surprise. She has a Father Christmas costume in her hands.*)

I wonder—could I learn that trick?

NICHOLAS. Have a go. Have a try, anyway. Just think hard, and blow.

NED. What. But it wouldn't . . . (*He makes a grimace of intense concentration, his eyes shut, and blows hard.*)

ANN (*moving above the settee in front of* NED). Are you going to be sick, Uncle Ned?

NED (*opening his eyes and looking angrily at* ANN). Damn it! You've spoilt it.

ANN. That trunk call to your friend—they're getting him for you now.

NED. Splendid! I'll come immediately. (*To* NICHOLAS.) And I'll be back in a minute for some more. (*He moves to the archway and turns.*) And, dammit, sir, you haven't given me an explanation of what you're doing in this house. Utterly nefarious—criminal and reprehensible. (*He scowls fiercely, then smiles happily.*) Show her the trick with the lamp, will you?

(NED *exits through the hall.*)

ANN. You seem to have made a—a friend of Uncle Ned, Mr Nicholas?

NICHOLAS. Magical, ain't it, miss? And how is little Cinderella?

ANN (*sitting at the* L. *end of the settee and putting the costume over her* R. *arm*). Cinderella's got her Prince.

NICHOLAS (*moving behind the settee* R. *of* ANN). That's fine. I'm doing well, ain't I?

ANN (*looking in front; sadly*). But he's the wrong Prince.

NICHOLAS. Dash me! Have I been mixing things up? That's the worst of being a careless magician. (*He pats her hair.*) Never mind, little lady, I'll try to put it right.

ANN. It would be won-der-ful if you could.

NICHOLAS. It isn't as easy as all that, you know. There's a bad fairy about—she isn't really a bad fairy, but she thinks she is one.

ANN. A bad fairy? (*She looks at him.*) Oh, you mean Aunt Topsey?

NICHOLAS. That's the lady's name.

ANN. Could you teach her a lesson, do you think?

NICHOLAS. Teaching lessons ain't my line. It's only people with no sense who like giving lessons—schoolmasters and school-mistresses—and they've got no sense at all. But we'll see what can be done.

(NED *enters through the hall.*)

NED (*moving down* R. *of the settee; shaking his head*). Don't think much of your telephone. Well, has he done any tricks for you?

ANN. No. But he's promised to do some.

NICHOLAS (*with a smile*). Some good 'uns. (*He moves to the* L. *of the settee.*)

NED (*looking at the costume*). Ah, so here it is. (*To* NICHOLAS.) My Father Christmas costume. I'll tell you what we'll do. We'll do a bit of magic—in collaboration—for the children at the convalescent home next door. We'll give them a ten-minute show after dinner, Mr —— Mr ——

NICHOLAS. Nicholas.

NED. Mr Nicholas.

ANN. Oh, they'd love that. But can Mr Nicholas *do* tricks?

NED. Can he do tricks. (*He moves up stage a little.*) See that lamp? Well, it was alight and he blew it out!

ANN. *Blew* it out?

NED. As easy as that. (*He takes a big breath, by way of demonstration, and puffs hard at the lamp, which immediately goes on.*)

ANN (*scared*). Oh!

NED (*dancing in wild excitement*). I've done it! (*He dances down stage* R.) I've done it! I'm damned if I know *how* I've done it—but I've done it.

NICHOLAS. Done it? You've done more than done it. I can blow a light out—but I've never seen anyone blow one on before.

NED. What a time we'll give the kids. What a time. (*To* NICHOLAS.) You're game?

NICHOLAS. Hold on a minute, sir. (*He moves a little down stage.*) One little matter we've forgotten. The lady—the dark lady who wanted to send for the police. I don't think she'd like my being . . .

NED (*moving towards the chair*). The mischief take her—that's true. (*He sits in the chair facing front.*)

ANN (*rising*). Look here, Uncle Ned. (*She moves towards* NED.) If Mr Nicholas were to slip up to the chauffeur's room, then Aunt Topsey would think that he'd gone, and he could meet you at the door of the Home.

NED. That's fine! (*He rises quickly.*) That's a grand idea.

NICHOLAS. That's very kind of you, miss.

ANN. If you go by the back stairs in about five minutes' time, no-one need see you. (*She moves towards the windows.*) It's getting dark. I'll draw the curtains. (*She draws the curtains and moves to the archway.*) And (*in a whisper to* NICHOLAS) you'll see what can be done about the right Prince, won't you?

NICHOLAS. You leave that to me.

ANN. Thank you, Mr Nicholas.

(ANN *exits up the stairs.*)

NED. The right Prince? (*He moves up* R. *and switches off the light.*)

(*The only light in the room is from the standard lamp.*)

What the devil's all that about? (*He moves to the armchair above the fireplace and takes his pipe from his pocket.*)

NICHOLAS. Just a little fairy story I was telling the young lady— a spot of trouble about the happy ending.

NED (*taking a box of matches from his pocket and lighting his pipe as he speaks*). What's that about a happy ending? (*He sits in the armchair.*)

NICHOLAS. The way a fairy story must finish, sir.

(*Children's voices are faintly heard singing a carol.*)

NED. More demon kings than fairy queens, I think. (*He puts the box of matches in his pocket.*)

NICHOLAS (*sitting at the* L. *end of the settee*). A little of each makes a world, sir. (*He takes his pipe from his pocket.*)

NED. Perhaps it does. (*He puffs at his pipe for a moment.*)

(NICHOLAS *watches him in silence.*)

So you believe—(*with an effort*) so you believe in the happy ending, do you?

NICHOLAS. You've got to believe in it, sir; else, where are you? (*He reaches for the matches on the table below the settee.*)

NED. Where are you indeed? (*He pauses.*) Heigh-ho. I'm not so far from my ending myself, and I don't know that it'll be such a happy one.

NICHOLAS (*lighting his pipe and tossing the box of matches on the table*). Ever speculate, sir, that an ending and a beginning are much the same thing?

NED. Don't think I follow you.

NICHOLAS (*puffing at his pipe*). Well, look at it this way, sir. Ever noticed how an old lady or an old gentleman seem to get on with a kiddy? It ain't just that *they* like the kiddy. The kiddy likes *them*. Sort of as though the very old and the very young had met at the end or the beginning of the circle. See what I mean? The old are just round their circle; the very young are just starting it—and they're together at the same point.

NED (*reflectively*). Never thought of it that way.

NICHOLAS. Ever ask yourself, sir, why Christmas is always represented by an old bloke with a long beard? *Old*, mark you. Yet Christmas stands for birth.

(*The carol is heard more loudly.*)

NED. I believe you've got a theory about life there.

NICHOLAS (*speaking slowly*). Maybe, I have, sir. Maybe, life is just a circle after all. You start at *A*, and round you go through the long curves of the years till you come to *A* again.

NED (*speaking thoughtfully and reflectively*). And then . . . ?

NICHOLAS. Maybe, you start off again on another circle—a higher one—doing your job.

NED. Your job?

NICHOLAS. The job you were given to do.

NED. You'd say, then, (*he draws at his pipe*) there is someone who sets the jobs?

NICHOLAS (*laughing quietly*). Bless your heart, sir. Have you any doubt about it? There's a plan in it all. These kids' voices—listen to them, sir, listen to them.

(*Both men sit listening while the carol swells out.* NED *is quietly beating time with his pipe. After a few moments the voices fade away.*)

NED. Yes—it's lovely, isn't it?

NICHOLAS. Lovely. And where do you think all that loveliness came from? And where do you think it goes to? Not lost, you know. Nothing's lost.

NED (*catching the other man's inflection*). I wonder? I remember once I was in a cathedral—Gloucester—it was the most beautiful of them all, I'd say. It was late in the afternoon. I seemed to be the only person in the place. And then I heard the organ playing very softly, and a boy's voice, that rang and rang round the pillars and arches like—like . . .

NICHOLAS (*whispering*). Like the Melody of God.

NED. That thought of yours struck me then. Where did it all come from? Where did it all go to?

NICHOLAS. It doesn't come or go, you know, sir. It's there all the time—if you have ears to hear it—the eyes to see it.

NED (*breaking the mood*). Sentimental old gentleman, I'm getting. (*He pauses.*) Being a bachelor's a lonely occupation, my friend.

NICHOLAS. You never gave a thought to marrying, sir?

NED. Oh, yes. And left it till it was too late.

NICHOLAS. It's never too late to mend, sir.

NED (*with some vigour*). Dammit! That's just what was in my mind. Are you at your thought-reading again?

NICHOLAS. I must have been.

NED. I wish . . .

(NICHOLAS *stretches his hands above his head, as though in a yawning moment, adding to the gesture of the right hand, an indication of command towards the door,* R.)

NICHOLAS. I have just wished, too. (*He rises and moves above the settee to the archway.*)

NED. Really. (*He rises.*) What?

NICHOLAS (*turning, by the Christmas tree*). Just that you should have your wish.

NED (*surprised*). But you've no idea what I . . .

NICHOLAS (*turning to exit through the hall, speaking as he goes*). None whatsoever, sir. But keep your eye on the door. Your wish might come through it.

(NICHOLAS *exits through the hall.*)

NED. Strange fellow. Still, no harm trying. (*He stands facing the door,* R.) I wish I had the courage to ask . . .

(*The door* R. *opens and* ENID *enters. She is holding her handbag.*)

ENID (*moving* R. *of the settee*). Well, Ned. What did you want to ask me?

NED (*very confused*). Why—I—I didn't—I did—Oh Lord! (*Moving below the* L. *end of the settee.*) Come and sit down, my dear.

(ENID *sits at the* R. *end of the settee.* NED *looks at her.*)

That's a lovely dress you're wearing.

Enid (*putting her handbag on the table below the settee*). You saw it yesterday.

Ned. Did I? And I didn't notice it? (*He sits at the* l. *end of the settee.*) It's there all the time, you know, if you have the eyes to see it.

Enid. What on earth are you saying, Ned?

Ned (*with genuine surprise in his voice*). What the devil *am* I saying?

Enid. I'm glad you like the dress, anyway.

Ned. Like it! Who could help but like it? You look—you look lovely, Enid.

Enid. Thanks. It is nice being told nice lies, isn't it? But, let's talk about you instead. How's the poor old lip?

Ned. The lip? Oh, yes, dammit, the lip. (*He takes the lipstick from his pocket and applies it to his lips.*) Yes. Good stuff, this. Makes it very comfortable. (*He puts the lipstick on the table below the settee and notices the pack of playing cards.*) Like me to show you some card tricks? (*He takes the cards in his hands.*)

Enid. Some *new* ones?

Ned (*throwing the cards on the table*). I haven't got any. Only the old ones—or—by Jove. (*He rises and faces the standard lamp.*) Watch the lamp—watch it carefully. (*He fills his lungs.*)

Enid. Yes, dear.

(Ned *blows a terrific puff at the lamp. Nothing whatever happens. He blows again, without result.*)

Enid (*puzzled and looking away from the lamp*). What is supposed to happen, Ned?

Ned (*a little puffed*). Well, if you want to know, I was trying to blow the lamp out.

Enid (*easily*). But, how silly, dear. Couldn't you use the switch?

Ned (*in anger and despair*). Couldn't you use the switch! Oh, women! Women! Can't you understand, Enid? It was a trick. (*He sits on the settee.*) But it's no use—I've forgotten the method.

Enid (*teasing him*). Did you ever know it? (*She takes her handbag from the table.*)

Ned (*in wrath*). Did I ever know it! Why (*suddenly deflated*) I don't believe I ever did. Dammit! I'm a silly old man. (*He picks up the playing cards.*)

Enid (*opening her handbag and taking out a compact and lipstick*). Not silly—and certainly not old. Did you have a nice time at Brighton? (*She replaces the handbag on the table.*)

Ned (*shuffling the cards*). Marvellous.

Enid. Good weather?

Ned. Yes. No. I mean—yes.

Enid. Which *do* you mean? (*She powders her nose.*)

Ned. I mean—dammit! (*He breaks off, unable to continue.*)

Enid. Damn it, indeed! Let's talk. (*She puts the compact and lipstick on the table.*)

Ned. What shall we talk about?

Enid. Ourselves. I haven't seen you for months.

Ned. Weeks—three weeks and four days, to be exact.

Enid (*softly*). So you remembered? Have you missed me a little?

Ned (*falling*). A little! Life's been one big hollow since I saw you.

Enid (*laughing a little*). You don't look too hollow, Ned.

Ned (*taking her hand*). Don't laugh at me, Enid.

(Topsey *enters from the hall and takes a few steps into the room.*)

If only you . . .

(Ned *draws* Enid *to him and their lips are about to meet. They do not notice that* Topsey *has entered.*)

Topsey (*moving down to* R. *of the settee; with a mirthless laugh*). Ha! Happy Christmas! Peace on earth.

Ned (*turning round; startled*). What the . . . ! (*He hastily breaks away from* Enid, *rises and moves to the fireplace.*)

Topsey. Goodwill towards *women*.

Ned. Where the devil did you spring from?

Topsey (*with asperity*). You know where you'll go if you keep on using bad language.

Ned (*furious*). Topsey Richards!

Topsey. What have you done with that burglar?

Ned. That's my business.

Topsey. It's my business, too. I don't want my throat cut in my sleep. (*She moves to the radiogram and collects her knitting.*)

Ned (*moving to* L. *of* Topsey). If I thought he would do that——

(Topsey *begins to retreat towards the archway.*)

—I'd give him the knife with my own hands. (*He advances towards her.*)

Topsey (*in the archway*). Ned Meldon! How dare you say such things to me? You ought to be ashamed of yourself!

Ned (*in terrific rage*). And what's more (*still advancing on her*) I'd clean up the mess with my own hands afterwards.

(Topsey *hastily exits through the hall.*)

(*Explosively.*) It's hard to believe that when that woman was born her mother gave birth to a baby. (*He moves behind and to the* L. *of the settee.*)

Enid. Never mind her. Come and sit down again.

Ned. Interfering mischief-making old faggot. (*He sits at the* L. *end of the settee.*)

ENID. Dear Ned. What a loyal friend you are.

NED. I wish I was twenty years younger.

ENID. And I wouldn't have a day off your age. For, if I did . . .

NED. Well? If you did . . . ?

ENID. Then you wouldn't have time to waste on an old frump like me.

NED. An old frump? My Heaven, Enid, when I look at you, what do I see? Something very precious—something *dear* beyond all cost.

ENID (*with a smile*). Yes, Ned. I expect you do. Make-up's horribly expensive nowadays.

NED. Don't put me off. And damn make-up. It's the real Enid I'm looking at—not a colour scheme.

ENID. I wonder how you'd like the real Enid without the colour scheme?

NED. I wonder how she likes me?

ENID. You know that already, Ned.

NED. Do I? By Jove! I wish I did. Enid, am I too old an old fool to . . .

ENID (*softly*). To what, Ned?

NED (*suddenly leaning back*). Oh! Oh Heaven! I'm going to faint. (*He puffs in some distress.*) My pulse's going at fifty miles an hour and I can't breathe.

ENID (*distressed*). Oh, Ned! Is it your heart?

NED (*emphatically*). *It is!* I feel like I felt before I got my first caning. I wish . . .

ENID. What!

NED (*all in a rush*). Enid, I love you. Will you—will you . . . ? (*He stops, summoning up courage.*)

ENID. If you were to take a deep breath, perhaps?

(ALICE *enters from the hall with tea things on a tray.*)

NED (*taking a huge breath*). Will you . . . ?

ALICE (*moving a few paces into the room*). Mind if I bring in the tea, Mr Edward?

NED. To hell with tea! (*He jumps up.*) What the devil do you mean by . . . ?

ENID (*not in the least flustered*). I'd no idea it was so late. (*She puts her compact in her handbag and closes it. She forgets all about her lipstick.*) I'll tell Mrs Meldon that tea's in, shall I, Alice? (*She rises and moves to the* L. *of* ALICE.)

ALICE. It'd be very kind of you if you would, madam. She's in her bedroom.

ENID. I will! (*She moves to the archway and turns to* NED.) You won't forget to finish telling me that story, will you, Ned?

(ENID *exits through the hall.*)

NED (*glaring at* ALICE). Alice, you're a damned fool!

ALICE. Well, how was I to know?

NED (*moving to the fireplace; angrily*). Know? Know what? What the devil are you insinuating?

ALICE (*moving to the table below the settee and putting down the tray*). I'm not insinuating anything, am I? And I've got to see you get your meals, haven't I? (*She moves to the archway.*)

NED (*contritely*). Sorry. Sorry, Alice. My damn quick temper. Forgive and forget.

ALICE (*in the archway*). Forgive and forget, indeed? That's just like a man. The woman forgives and the man forgets. If I were the Creator, I'd give the men the memories.

NED. What would you give the women?

ALICE. The trousers!

(ALICE *exits through the hall.*)

NED. Oh! I asked for that. (*He looks serious for a moment, then grins to himself. He feels in his pocket for his pipe and puts it in his mouth. He immediately takes it out, rubs his lips and looks at them in the mirror over the fireplace.*) Shingles! (*He feels hastily in his pocket for the lipstick and cannot find it.*) Dammit! Where's it gone to? (*He looks in his pockets again, crosses to the settee and looks hopefully on it. Suddenly he finds the lipstick on the table below the settee. Although he does not know it, it is* ENID's *lipstick he picks up. He sits on the settee and proceeds to rub the lipstick vigorously on and above his lips. It is a bright pillar-box shade. He now has a crimson circle around his mouth. All unconscious of this he completes the job.*) That's better. (*He replaces the lipstick in his pocket and smiles to himself. Then he looks round the room. He notices the writing table.*) Ah! (*He rises, moves to the writing table and sits in the chair. He takes a piece of notepaper and begins to write.*) "My dearest Enid, . . ."

(*He continues writing as* MARY *enters the room through the hall.* ANN *comes down the stairs.*)

MARY (*to* ANN). Hello, darling! Where's everybody?

(ALICE *is heard ringing a gong off* R. ANN *comes into the room.*)

Ah, that'll bring them. Ann, pour out, will you?

(ANN *moves to the settee, sits and begins to pour out the tea.*)

Oh, Ned . . . ! (*She moves to the* R. *of the settee.*)

NED (*without turning round*). Yes, my dear?

MARY. If you want stamps they're in the drawer.

NED (*still without turning round*). No, darling. Oh!—(*He is embarrassed.*) I mean—no, Mary. I shan't need any stamps for *this* letter.

(MARY *looks at* ANN *and* ANN *offers her a cup of tea which she takes to* NED. *She is about to put the cup of tea down on the table beside him.*)

(*Deep in writing.*) Thanks. Thanks. (*He turns round fully to her.*)

(MARY *sees his face and recoils.*)

MARY (*still holding the tea; in horror*). Oh! (*Her hand shakes the cup.*)

(ANN *rises quickly and moves to* MARY.)

NED. What's wrong? What's wrong? Dammit, you've spilt the tea.

ANN. What is it, Mother? (*She suddenly sees* NED's *face and cannot resist a giggle.*)

NED. That's right, Ann. Laugh and the world laughs with you. And it's a grand old world.

MARY (*weakly*). I'll—I'll get you another cup. (*She moves to the settee, sits, and prepares to pour out another cup of tea.*)

NED (*returning to his writing*). Yes, I could do with a nice cup of tea.

(ANN *helps* MARY *with the tea.* TONY *enters through the door* R.)

TONY (*moving to the* L. *of* NED). I suppose you're right about tea?
NED. Of course I am.
TONY. I'm not so sure. Afternoon tea on Christmas Day is a tactical error. One should keep one's stomach empty for the Great Event.

ANN (*handing a cup of tea to* NED *and moving behind the settee, trying not to look at him*). Here you are, Uncle Ned.

(MARY *rises and tries to attract* TONY's *attention.* TONY *takes no notice.*)

NED. Not at all, my boy, you're wrong. And, to prove it, I'll have a sandwich.

TONY (*moving to the table below the settee*). A sandwich for Uncle Ned. (*He takes a plate from the table and offers it to* NED.)

(NED *turns round.* TONY *sees his face.*)

Gosh! (*He drops the plate.*)

(ANN *moves* L. *of the settee to* MARY.)

NED (*a little warmly*). What's wrong with everyone in this house? You've all got nerves.

TONY (*hastily retrieving the sandwiches and returning to the table, his eyes one big question mark*). Oh, nothing, Uncle Ned.

(MARY *whispers to* ANN *and urges her towards* NED. *Unaware that the others know of the condition of* NED's *lips,* TONY *tries to indicate it to them by gesture. They take no notice.*)

(*He commences to sing and points to* NED.) *Red sails in the Sunset.*

(MARY *gives* ANN *a final push.* TONY *moves above the* R. *end of the settee.*)

ANN. Why is it always me? (*She picks up another plate of sandwiches and with her handkerchief in her hand moves reluctantly towards* NED.)

NED (*turning to face her and taking a sandwich*). Thanks, Ann.

ANN (*taking her handkerchief*). Uncle Ned. You've got a tiny —a tiny little mark on your lip. Let me—let me take it off for you.

NED. My lip? What's wrong with my lip? It isn't a mark, it's my shingles. Damn it, Mary, this stuff of yours can't be working. Haven't I—(*he is feeling in his pockets*) haven't I got enough on? (*He finds the lipstick and begins to apply more.*)

ANN. Oh, no! No! Uncle Ned.

NED. I hope that'll do the trick.

ANN (*with a glance at him*). It has.

(NED *puts the lipstick in his pocket and returns to his writing.* ANN *moves below the settee with the plate.* GEORGE *enters from the hall, and moves below the Christmas tree.* ANN *sees him and hastily moves* L. *of the settee towards him. She grabs hold of his arm and pulls him to the armchair above the fireplace.*)

Have a sandwich, quickly, and sit down *there.* (*She pushes him into the armchair.*)

GEORGE (*collapsing into the chair*). Well, I'll say your English hospitality is positively overpowering.

MARY (*moving quickly to the* L. *of* GEORGE). Yes. I expect you find everything rather strange over here, George.

GEORGE. Aw, well, there *are* some funny things.

ANN. Well (*returning to the table*) if you see anything funny, don't laugh at it.

(NED, *having finished his letter, rises and faces them.*)

NED (*disapprovingly*). That's a strange thing to say, Ann. I don't agree with you at all.

(GEORGE *looks up and sees him.*)

If you see anything funny, my boy, laugh at it as much as you can —provided it *is* funny.

GEORGE (*bursting into laughter*). Ha!—Ha!—Ha!

(ANN *rushes to* GEORGE *and hastily puts a hand over his mouth.* NED, *absent-mindedly, strokes his lips, spreading the lipstick over his cheek.* GEORGE *frees himself, and, with a wild gesture, pointing at* NED, *collapses into uncontrollable laughter.* NED *glares at him, unconsciously touching his lips again.*)

NED. Well, I'm damned! You infernal, ill-mannered young cub. Are you laughing at me?

(GEORGE *nods hysterically.*)

(*He moves* R. *of the settee.*) I tell you, I'll stand this no longer. (*He looks round at the others.*) I ask you—I ask you all . . .

(ANN *titters.* NED *glares at her.* TONY, *abandoning himself, laughs out-right and moves* R. *of* GEORGE. *Finally,* MARY *succumbs, and they all lean back laughing.*)

(*Trying to keep control of himself.*) Mary! (*Loudly.*) Mary Meldon!
    MARY. I can't help it, Ned. You look so funny. (*She goes off into a peal of laughter.*)

(TOPSEY *enters from the hall. A dead silence falls, as all fear the worst.*)

NED (*now bursting with rage*). I see! I see! I understand. This is a practical joke. (*He turns away and moves a little down* R.)
    TOPSEY (*as though resenting it*). Well, what is the joke? (*She moves down a few paces.*)
    NED (*his back half-turned to* TOPSEY, *speaking with fearful dignity*). The joke, which I am glad you cannot see, Topsey Richards, was . . (*He turns to her.*)

TOPSEY *gazes at him in astonishment, her determined little face more ill-tempered than ever. Then, without the slightest warning, she puts her hands on her hips, leans backwards and shrieks uncontrollably with laughter. This is too much for the others, who break in with hysterical laughter again.* NED *brings his hand to his mouth and suddenly with horror notices the lipstick on his fingers. It then dawns on him that the lipstick must be the cause of the laughter. And while everyone is still roaring with laughter——*

the CURTAIN *quickly falls.*

ACT III

SCENE.—*The same. About six o'clock on Christmas evening. All the lights are on but the curtains are drawn. The standard lamp has now been placed in its original position.*

As the CURTAIN *rises, the wireless is playing Roger Quilter's "Children's Overture". ANN is sitting on the arm of the armchair above the fireplace, listening to it. She is smoking. Her handbag is in the armchair. After a moment,* MARY *enters from the hall with some parcels in her hands. She moves to the table below the settee and deposits her parcels on it.*

ANN (*rising*). Can I help?

MARY. No, thanks. You might draw the curtains, though.

ANN (*looking at the windows*). Do you mind if I keep them as they are? (*She looks at* MARY.) The snow looks so lovely. (*She moves to the wireless and switches it off.*)

MARY (*moving to the* R. *of* ANN). Sentimental child. (*She glances at* ANN.) Ann, I'm sure you're smoking too much. You'll become a slave to it.

ANN. Nonsense, Mother. I could give it up quite easily, if I wanted to, but . . .

(TONY *enters from the hall. He has a few very small parcels in his hands.*)

TONY. But you never want to. (*He moves a few paces into the room.*)

MARY (*to* TONY). Tony, have you—er—seen Uncle Ned since —since the . . .

TONY (*with a gesture, moving to the table below the settee and putting his parcels on it*). The foot and mouth disease? No—but I've heard him.

MARY. Heard him?

TONY. Yes—singing.

ANN (*returning to the armchair above the fireplace*). Singing?

TONY (*moving to the writing table*). In his bath. Does he have to have a bath to get lipstick off his lips? (*He sits at the writing table.*)

ANN (*sitting on the arm of the armchair; bitterly*). He hasn't had your experience, Tony!

(TONY *begins to write a label for a parcel.*)

MARY (*moving to the* L. *of* TONY). Did you notice *what* he was singing?

TONY. "Onward Christian Soldiers, marching as to WAR!"

MARY. Oh, dear.

Tony. There'll be war all right, and heaven help the non-combatants! (*He takes a cigarette from the box on the writing table, picks up the label, rises and moves to* Ann.) Give me a light, will you?

(Ann *takes her handbag, opens it and takes out a lighter.*)

You're getting on very nicely with this George fellow, aren't you?
Ann. Well?

(Mary *sits at the writing table and writes a label.*)

Tony. Oh, very well. Fast work. Keep your speed up round the corners and you'll catch your electric hare.
Ann (*handing* Tony *the lighter*). Thanks for the advice, To-ny.
Tony (*lighting his cigarette and handing the lighter to* Ann). Not at all. It's your cup of tea, of course. Though (*with vigour*) what you can see in that grinning, half-baked moron, I'm damned if I can see. (*He moves to the* R. *of the table below the settee, and begins to tie the label on to a parcel.*)
Ann (*indignantly*). George isn't a moron! (*Curiously.*) What is a moron, Tony?
Tony (*uncertainly*). A moron is—well, it's—it's a sort of—anyway, George is a moron.
Ann. I'll tell him you said so.
Tony. Christmas presents seem to be doing well. Here's my little lot.
Ann (*glancing at them*). They're certainly a *little* lot.
Tony (*loftily*). It's not the money that counts, but the thought. (*He moves to the fireplace.*)

(Olivia *enter from the hall.*)

Olivia (*moving a few paces into the room*). Heard the latest?
Tony. No! What?
Olivia (*moving between the chair and settee*). Uncle Ned. The weather's changed. Further outlook, favourable. Wind from the west again. The entire country is enjoying summer conditions.
Mary (*rising, crossing to the table below the settee and tring her label on to a parcel*). What *are* you talking about, Olivia?
Olivia (*moving behind the settee towards* Ann). Uncle Ned. He's up with daddy in his room. Roars of laughter from them both. He's telling daddy all about the lipstick tragedy. They're nearly in hysterics about it. And he's trying on his Christmas costume.
Mary (*with a sigh of relief*). That is good news! He's got over it then? Maybe now we shall have a little peace! (*She sits on the settee.*)
Tony (*moving down* L.). Peace! At Christmas? With Uncle Ned in the house? What an optimist?

(Alice *enters from the hall and moves between the chair and the settee.*)

Mary. I don't think anything else is likely to go astray, Tony.
Alice. Don't you, ma'am?

MARY. What is it, Alice? Nothing wrong, I hope?
ALICE. Nothing wrong! Oh, nothing. Just that you won't none
of you get any Christmas dinner.

(MARY *and* ANN *rise.*)

MARY
ANN
TONY   } (*together*). What!
OLIVIA

ALICE. The boiler's begun to leak—it's bust!
MARY. Alice!
TONY. And to think I deliberately avoided having any tea.
MARY. Oh, my Heavens! What *will* we do? Are you sure, Alice?
ALICE (*moving towards the archway*). Come and look for yourself.

(MARY *follows* ALICE *to the archway. They are about to exit when*
GEORGE *enters through the hall. He looks radiant.*)

TONY. Can we . . . ?
MARY. For Heaven's sake, stay where you are, all of you!
Now, Alice—hello, George!

(MARY *and* ALICE *exit through the hall.*)

GEORGE (*very heartily indeed*). Well, gee! (*He moves in front of the
Christmas tree.*) I think England at Christmas is just grand. Grand
place, England. Grand time, Christmas.
TONY (*flopping in the armchair down* L.). Leave him to his dreams
and his empty stomach.
OLIVIA. Where have you been, George? I was—I was looking
for you.
GEORGE (*casually*). I took a stroll. Working up an appetite for
dinner—what Tony calls the Great Event.
OLIVIA. George! It looks as though there isn't going to be—a
Great Event.
GEORGE. Say! What d'you mean?
ANN (*sitting in the armchair above the fireplace*). There isn't going
to be any Christmas dinner. The boiler's burst.
GEORGE (*very anxiously*). Aw! You're joking, aren't you?
OLIVIA (*moving slowly to the front of the settee*). It's all too true.
The boiler's leaking so we'll have to put out the kitchen fire.
GEORGE. Gee! That's awful, isn't it? Can't you get it mended
quick?
OLIVIA (*sitting on the* L. *of the settee*). This is Christmas Day, and
there'll be no-one working till Thursday.
GEORGE (*moving to the* R. *of the settee; angrily*). Now, I ask you.
The boiler bursts on a Monday and no-one will work till Thurs-
day. (*He sits on the arm of the settee.*) Dear old, antiquated England.
What a country to live in.

OLIVIA. Only a miracle will have the kitchen fire going inside a week.

ANN (*suddenly*). Only a *miracle?*

TONY. And *they* don't happen—not even (*with a look at* GEORGE) in dear old, up-to-date Canada.

ANN. I wonder—I wonder . . . (*She suddenly rises, moves behind the settee and leans across to* GEORGE.) George, dear . . .

GEORGE (*reacting*). Yes, sweetheart?

(TONY *registers an expression of disgust.*)

ANN. I want you to go across to the gar-age and see (*speaking very impetuously*) and see if you could find Mr Nicholas. Tell him about the boiler—and ask him if he could do anything about it.

GEORGE (*rising*). Sure I will. (*He moves to the* L. *of the archway.*) Wonderful country, this. The boiler bursts and the only person who can mend it is a burglar. Well!

TONY (*rising and moving above the settee to the* R. *of* GEORGE). If you haven't a nice little job for me, Ann, I'll go and join the boiler party. (*To* GEORGE.) If you could spare a little of your chewing-gum? This *is* going to be an austerity Christmas.

(GEORGE *exits through the hall.* TONY, *with a look at* ANN, *follows him.* OLIVIA *rises and moves to the writing table. She takes a cigarette from the box, lights it and registers strong disapproval of* ANN's *tactics.*)

OLIVIA. Anyway, *you're* having a Happy Christmas, little sister.

ANN (*moving to the* L. *of the settee*). I am! Ooh—I *am.*

OLIVIA. Funny to see *you* ordering two men about, isn't it?

ANN. I'm sure *you* find it funny, Olivia.

OLIVIA. Don't think I haven't seen through your little game. You're making baby eyes at George just because you think I want your Tony.

ANN. *My* Tony? Oh, not *my* Tony. (*She sits at the* L. *end of the settee.*) My George, perhaps.

OLIVIA. Ann!

ANN. Yes—*dear?*

OLIVIA. Supposing we—supposing we call it a day? This Tony and George business?

ANN. I like it as it is, thanks.

OLIVIA (*moving to the* R. *of the settee*). For Heaven's sake, talk sense. If you want your wretched Tony, you can have him. I never met such a young bore in my life.

ANN (*angrily*). He's not a bore!

OLIVIA. Of course he is. (*She moves below the* R. *end of the settee.*) Only you're clever enough not to show him that he bores you.

ANN. Olivia!

OLIVIA (*sitting at the* R. *end of the settee*). It's silly quarrelling over two men when we can each have either of them.

Ann. You told me . . . (*She rises; a little angry.*) You actually told me you were going to *practise* on Tony.

Olivia. Well, my gosh! Haven't you been practising on George?

Ann. He seems to like it. (*She moves to the fireplace and stands with her back to* Olivia.) So—so do I. (*She giggles.*)

Olivia. Isn't it enough that I've said that you can have Tony back?

Ann (*turning*). No (*with emphasis*) it isn't!

Olivia. Why not?

Ann. I don't know that I want Tony back.

Olivia. God knows, *I* don't want him.

Ann. I don't know that I could persuade George to go back to *you*.

Olivia. You dare to tell me that . . . ?

Ann. Well, he's got ac-customed to a higher standard now.

Olivia (*rising*). You little beast. You little mischief-maker. In the Middle Ages you'd be living in the stocks.

Ann. And in the Middle Ages you'd be living in a cage.

(Aunt Topsey *enters from the hall and stands in the archway. She has her knitting and some wool in one hand and her handbag in the other.*)

Olivia. Oh! (*She flounces towards the archway straight into the arms of* Topsey.)

Topsey. Be careful, will you! Where are you off to—like the *Flying Scotsman?*

Olivia (*furiously*). Scotland!

(Olivia *disentangles herself from* Topsey *and exits through the hall.* Topsey *looks after* Olivia, *in mingled rage and astonishment.*)

Topsey (*moving to the* R. *end of the settee*). Your mother wants you, Ann. (*With a nod towards the archway.*) What on earth's the matter with *her?*

Ann. You're asking *me?*

Topsey (*putting her·wool and knitting on the settee; irately*). Of course I'm asking you. What do you think I'm doing?

Ann (*moving above the* L. *end of the settee*). Do you believe in miracles, Aunt Topsey?

Topsey. No, I don't! Why?

Ann. I didn't—but I'm beginning to. (*She moves to the archway.*)

Topsey (*moving up* R.). Don't talk such absurd nonsense. And don't try to evade my question. You know perfectly well I asked you what was wrong with your sister. (*She puts her handbag on the settee.*)

Ann (*magnanimously*). Oh, you mustn't blame her. It's my fault really. I've burst her boiler.

(Ann *exits through the hall.* Topsey *snorts indignantly, then moves to the table below the settee and looks at the presents.*)

Topsey (*with contempt*). Christmas presents! Sentimental rubbish! (*She picks up her handbag, takes out some envelopes and throws them down quickly on to the table, reading the inscriptions as she does so.*) Mary, from Topsey. Ned, from Topsey. Olivia, from Aunt Topsey. Ann, from Aunt Topsey, Enid, from Topsey. Alice, from Topsey. (*She laughs as she reads the last envelope.*) Topsey, from Topsey.

(Topsey *turns away from the table and looks around the room. She moves to the radiogram, switches it on and moves to the armchair above the fireplace. From the radiogram can now be heard the "Blue Danube". She turns the armchair a little to face the fire, moves to the settee, picks up her knitting and handbag and returns to the armchair. She sits in the armchair, puts her handbag by her side and proceeds to knit. The music grows louder. The door R. opens and* Ned *enters, wearing his Father Christmas beard. Thinking himself alone and caught by the music, he does a pirouette or two with an imaginary partner.* Topsey *does not hear his entrance owing to the music. He approaches the standard lamp, looks at it, takes a deep breath and blows at it.* Topsey *half looks round, though he has made little noise. Nothing happens to the light. He shrugs his shoulders and moves behind the settee.* Nicholas *enters from the hall and stands in the archway watching* Ned, *who is now rather peevishly and carelessly blowing an angry puff at the chandelier.* Nicholas, *seeing his chance, immediately moves to the switch and turns off the light. The only illumination is from the standard lamp.* Topsey *immediately gives a vigorous scream.* Nicholas *disappears through the hall.*)

Ned (*with emotion and all in one word*). God bless my soul.
Topsey (*jumping up*). Ned! What are you playing at now?
Ned (*still a little aghast at his work*). I wish I knew.
Topsey. Turn on the light at once.

(Ned *moves to the switch, fiddles with it, and the light comes on.*)

Ned (*after a pause*). Topsey. I came in to—to herry the batchet.
Topsey (*annoyance and mystification in her voice*). To what?
Ned (*moving above the settee*). To herry the batchet—bury the hatchet, I mean.
Topsey (*uncompromisingly*). Oh, did you?
Ned. Topsey, can't we start all over again and be friends? This is Christmas, dammit.
Topsey. So you're damning Christmas now, are you? That's nice.
Ned (*moving to the* L. *of the settee and controlling himself with great effort*). I'm sorry. But it seems all wrong we should have to quarrel on *this* day of all days. I'm willing to . . .
Topsey (*interrupting*). I can't hear a word while you have that silly thing on your face.

NED (*with a calm that is almost ominous in its completeness*). I'll take it off, Topsey. (*He takes off the beard.*)

TOPSEY. You look less like a nanny-goat now. Well?

NED. I'm trying to say, Topsey, that we ought to make up our little quarrels on Christmas Day.

TOPSEY (*with vigour*). Sentimental rubbish! You're old enough to know better.

NED. Time marches on for both of us, Topsey—but we needn't make it a quick march.

TOPSEY. Fiddlesticks! Have you no sense? Spending your last years making a fool of yourself. (*She moves the standard lamp nearer to the armchair.*)

NED. You think I'm making a fool of myself? And that I'm too—too old to think of—well—of making a change in my life?

TOPSEY. You know the answer to that yourself. You can't teach an old dog young tricks.

NED (*sadly*). Maybe you're right. (*He sighs deeply.*) An old, old dog. (*He moves to sit on the settee.*)

TOPSEY. Of course I'm right. And don't sit on my wool. (*She moves in front of the fireplace.*)

NED. Sorry, Topsey. I'm sorry for disturbing you. I'll leave you in peace. (*He is about to move up* R.)

TOPSEY (*abruptly*). Get me a chair.

NED. A chair? Certainly. (*He takes hold of the chair and puts it down facing her.*)

TOPSEY (*angrily*). Good Heavens! The man's got no sense. Not that way. *That* way!

NED (*suddenly flashing into wrath*). Dammit! What way d'you want it? There's no pleasing you. (*He turns the chair round.*) Sorry again, Topsey. Got everything you want? (*He moves to the archway and ruefully shakes his head at her.*) "Yes, thank you, dear Uncle Ned, and I wish you a Happy Christmas".

(TOPSEY *snorts indignantly and arranges the wool on the chair.* NED *is about to exit when* NICHOLAS *enters from the hall.*)

NICHOLAS. Good evening, all.

NED (*heartily*). Hello, Mr Nicholas. (*In a stage whisper.*) Got any more magic up your sleeve, eh?

NICHOLAS. Might have, sir.

NED (*clasping his hands in front of him in a theatrical gesture and suddenly opening them; with a conspirators air, towards* TOPSY). Do you think you could make *her* vanish? For God's sake, *try*.

(NED, *with a friendly grin at* NICHOLAS, *exits through the hall.*)

TOPSEY. You might as well put out that light. (*She sits in the armchair above the fireplace.*)

NICHOLAS (*with a smile to himself*). What! Again? (*He is about to blow it out, then thinks better of it, switches off the light, then advances into the room and looks at* TOPSEY. *Moving below the settee.*) Good evening.

TOPSEY. What are you doing here still?

NICHOLAS. I'm just waiting.

TOPSEY. Waiting for what?

NICHOLAS. For something to happen to someone.

TOPSEY. Well, go and wait somewhere else. I don't know why you're allowed to stay in the house at all after breaking into it.

NICHOLAS. Aaaar! Once I gets in, I'm hard to get rid of. That's the best of me. (*He grins to himself ruefully.*) But getting in's a hard job sometimes. People shuts you out.

TOPSEY. I should think so, indeed.

NICHOLAS (*moving to the chair and looking on it*). Bless my heart!

TOPSEY (*looking up; angry*). What is it?

NICHOLAS. Oh! Only just my fancy. (*He breaks off and looks pensively at* TOPSEY.) Wonderful thing, imagination.

TOPSEY. Rubbish!

NICHOLAS. Oh, no, ma'am, not rubbish. (*He pauses.*) Wonderful thing what imagination does to you. What it does *for* you. (*His voice is dreamy now.*) Like a kid's—you know. Bit of dust dancing in the light of a dull, old room. Box of geraniums in the windows of number ninety Shabby Street. (*He quietens his voice to a gradual whisper.*) Smell of the smoke from a train going somewhere—going somewhere—we're all of us faring somewhere, aren't we? Even though we seem to be staying still. (*He stares down at the chair and suddenly raises his voice.*) Jimminy-Josephey!

TOPSEY (*angrily*). What is it *now*?

NICHOLAS. Imagination, of course. But I'll swear I saw someone sitting in that chair.

TOPSEY (*annoyed and angry*). What!

NICHOLAS (*quite unperturbed and very definitely*). There was someone sitting in that chair—quite a young fellow. (*As though asking himself the question.*) What age would you say? Twenty-five or thirty?

TOPSEY. Look here . . .

NICHOLAS. In uniform—officer's uniform—but old-fashioned-like. A tall fellow.

TOPSEY. What are you talking about? (*Her voice is gruff, but it lacks its usual confidence.*) You really think you saw someone there? Ridiculous!

NICHOLAS. Not saw, ma'am—*imagined.* Imagined him quite plain. Brown hair he had with a wave in it.

TOPSEY (*suddenly*). What are you saying?

NICHOLAS. He'd a brown moustache, and—and . . .

TOPSEY. What trick's this?

NICHOLAS (*softly*). No trick, ma'am.

TOPSEY (*almost as though afraid*). Did you . . . ? (*She breaks off.*)

NICHOLAS. Did I—notice anything else about him? (*Very softly.*) I did, ma'am.

TOPSEY (*softly*). What?

NICHOLAS. On his finger was a big signet ring——

(TOPSEY'S *hand, with an imperceptible movement, covers the ring on her own finger.*)

—a big signet ring, with the letter R set in a green, flat stone. And, do you know what he was doing, this young man? He was sitting on this chair—across it. (*He straddles himself across the chair and gently takes the wool in his hand.*) And he was holding the wool for you—this way.

(TOPSEY *quietly stops rolling the wool. She does not look at him.*)

It'd be strange, ma'am (*his voice is a gentle whisper now*) it'd be strange if you'd ever known someone—someone who'd held your wool for you—like this—someone in an old-fashioned uniform, who wore a signet ring—it'd be strange, wouldn't it, ma'am, if you'd ever known someone who'd sat like this.

(TOPSEY, *with a slight effort, brings herself to look at him.*)

TOPSEY (*unsteadily*). Yes—it would be strange. (*She commences to roll the wool again from his hands.*)

NICHOLAS. And strange, too, if I said something that reminded you of what someone else had said, when *he* was sitting—like this —and holding the wool.

(*The wool sticks on a corner of the chair.* TOPSEY *automatically puts out a hand to free it, but* NICHOLAS, *with a gesture, looks at her. Then, with a movement of his arms, frees the wool and speaks in an only just audible whisper, but with meaning in his voice.*)

"Here we go round the Mulberry Tree."

(TOPSEY *puts down the ball of wool very quietly and looks, with an effort, at* NICHOLAS.)

Perhaps *he* was here all the time. (*Again there is meaning in his voice.*) Perhaps he's been sitting here—thinking the things I'm thinking . . . (*He breaks off.*)

(TOPSEY *waits for him to continue, then, as he does not, she speaks again in a low, strange voice.*)

TOPSEY. What *are* you thinking?

(NICHOLAS *does not immediately reply. When he does so, his tones are the same as before, but he speaks as though to himself.*)

NICHOLAS. Long ago and now—coming and going, but here all the time—like Christmas, you know—like Christmas. (*He

*E

pauses.) Empty chair—chair like this one. And someone in it holding the wool.

(TOPSEY'S *hands pause over her wool as he says this*.)

Was he telling her something? Something she'd dreaded hearing —though she sort-of knew she'd have to hear it some time?— That his regiment was going overseas—and that—that he mightn't come back? From that war so many—*didn't* come back. And if he didn't come back—she was just to go on being her old self—brave-like—not changing a bit. Not getting bitter and sour —being as she'd always been to him—thoughtful—understanding —gentle . . . (*He stops again*.)

(TOPSEY *seems afraid to speak for a moment*.)

TOPSEY. And she?
NICHOLAS. Crying, she was—crying.

(TOPSEY, *with an effort, throws down her wool and rises to her feet. She moves to the fireplace and stands there with her back half turned to* NICHOLAS.)

Lumme! (*Still softly*.) How we try to deceive ourselves, don't we? We say to ourselves "The world's been hard and bitter—it's taken it out of me. I'll be hard and bitter, and take it out of the world." But, can we? Not on your life, you can't. There's always some little thing that's got to be done for folk who ain't able to do it for themselves. And you always do it. Hard and bitter or not, you always do it.

TOPSEY (*speaking with difficulty*). Why are you telling me this?
NICHOLAS (*appearing to come out of his reverie, rising and moving* L. *of the settee*). Bless you, ma'am. Was I talking to myself? Shocking bad habit, that. Comes of being a bachelor. A poor old bachelor like—(*he appears to be thinking for a second and speaks as though the idea had only just occurred to him*) like Mr Ned. Will *he* go on being a bachelor till the end of his days? (*He smiles to himself*.) There's my old imagination starting up again! I was thinking poor Mr Ned would never pluck up courage enough to ask the lady he wants to ask. And then, old imagination pops on and asks, "Suppose someone else took a hand and asked the question for him?" (*He laughs*.) Who'd do that? I ask you. Who'd do a crazy thing like that? (*Dropping his voice to a confidential whisper*.) Why, I suppose someone who was thoughtful—and understanding—and gentle.

(TOPSEY *turns and moves slowly in front of the settee to the archway*.)

Someone who didn't change—who went on being her old self, brave-like.

(TOPSEY *is in the archway now and* NICHOLAS *knows she is, though he does not look up in her direction*.)

Someone who wanted—who wanted—(*his voice takes on command and something near to benediction*) a Happy Christmas.

(TOPSEY *exits through the hall.* NICHOLAS *turns to watch her go. He then puts the chair in front of the writing table and deposits the wool on the radiogram, half singing, half speaking to himself as he does so.*)

I shot an arrow into the air; it fell to earth, I know not where. But (*the comment is spoken to himself*)—I've a very good idea where.

(NED *enters from the hall. He switches on the light and gazes round the room.*)

NED. You haven't really made her disappear, have you?

NICHOLAS. Only the wrong half of her, sir.

NED (*moving to the Christmas tree*). What?

NICHOLAS (*moving to the fireplace*). What am I saying? Oh, no. Miss Topsey hasn't disappeared. You'll be hearing from her again—and at second hand, too.

NED (*moving above the* L. *end of the settee*). What on earth do you mean?

NICHOLAS. Forgive me, sir. I'm harmless, really. That kitchen boiler and I have just the same trouble.

NED. What's that?

NICHOLAS. Screw loose, sir.

NED (*laughing*). Damn good! Damn good! And you put that boiler to rights in double-quick time, eh?

NICHOLAS. Yes, sir. I've put a lot of things to rights in this house. (*The remark strikes* NICHOLAS *as being funny and he doubles up with laughter.*) Oh, my ribs. (*He blows out heavily in an involuntary fashion and the standard lamp immediately goes out.*)

NED. Good Lord, Mr Nicholas. I'd give my eyes on sticks to know how you do that.

NICHOLAS. Well, sir, I'll give you a hint to start with. You see some electric wall plugs (*with a nod of his head towards the plug in question*) are stuck in a bit loose and if you given them a little pressure with your foot, which nobody notices just as you blow—why, then, the trick's done.

NED. Oh! (*He sounds crestfallen.*) Is that all there is in it? I was hoping (*he sounds a little ashamed*) there was something—something, well, a bit magical about . . .

NICHOLAS (*interrupting*). Ah, maybe you're right, sir. Maybe there *is* a bit of magic in it all the same. It all depends how you blow. You've got to blow hard. (*He puffs.*) Like that. But not too hard, or you might blow yourself away. (*He looks at the chandelier and takes a huge breath then blows, aiming the breath at the chandelier.*)

(*The chandelier promptly goes out.* NICHOLAS *quickly disappears into the hall and up the stairs.*)

NED. That's hot! By jove, that's hot. (*He moves to the switch.*)

But I did it myself this afternoon. (*He switches on the light.*) And I wasn't trying very hard, either. Look here, Mr Nicholas. (*He pauses. He is a little perturbed and looks round the room, calling.*) Mr Nicholas! (*He begins to search behind the curtains.*) Dammit! This is a bit too much of a good thing! Mr Nicholas . . .

(ENID *enters from the hall. She moves to* NED *at the window. She is happy and excited.*)

ENID. Ned, Ned! You absurd old darling. Of course the answer is *Yes*.

NED (*still busy looking for* NICHOLAS *behind the curtains; vaguely*). Yes? Oh, that's all right. Another time, my dear. I'm busy now. Lost something?

ENID (*with disappointment and astonishment in her voice*). Ned! I didn't think you—you would send me a message like that by Topsey unless you . . . (*She breaks off and moves towards the archway.*)

NED (*still busy*). Message! Dammit! Where has the man hidden himself? (*He vaguely looks up at* ENID.) What message by Topsey?

ENID (*sadly*). Only that you wanted to marry me.

NED (*stupidly*). Only that *what*? (*In an excited shout.*) What!

(*He dashes across the room towards* ENID *as she is about to exit.*)

Come back! Come back!

(ENID *pauses.*)

Topsey gave you that message from me?

ENID. Yes.

NED (*in wild excitement*). Bless her heart. Bless her heart. And the answer is, Yes!

ENID. Yes—if you mean it, Ned.

NED. If I mean it! If I mean it! Whoops! (*He takes her in his arms and kisses her wildly.*)

(*As he does so,* ALICE *appears in the archway. She takes in the situation at a glance and, without a word, wheels and begins to exit.* NED, *seeing this, calls after her.*)

Alice! Alice! Come back and congratulate us.

ALICE (*turning*). I congratulate you. Eat, drink, and be married, for tomorrow you die.

(*As* ALICE *turns to exit* MARY *enters from the hall.*)

MARY. Congratulations, indeed.

(NED *breaks away above the writing table.* ALICE *exits through the hall.* MARY *takes* ENID *above the* L. *end of the settee.*)

NED. Thanks, Mary. Where's Topsey? Where's Topsey? *I must* go and thank her.

Mary. She's not coming down for the presents, but she is going over to the Home with us.

Ned. Oh! Don't tell the others yet—keep it as a surprise.

(Ann *enters from the hall, with* George. *He is carrying a tray with parcels on it.*)

Bless you, Ann, my child. Bless you. (*He rushes up to* Ann *and, without the least warning, embraces her.*)

(George *watches; surprised.*)

(*He turns to* George.) And, George—*dear* old George.

George (*terrified he is going to be kissed*). Aw—look here, sir. (*He backs away and nearly crashes into the Christmas tree.*)

Ned (*turning to* Ann). Dear little Ann—my favourite god-daughter.

Ann. Was I a good godchild?

Ned. I was a good godfather! I never cried once. (*He crosses in front of the settee to the fireplace.*)

(George *moves to the table in front of the settee.* Ann *follows, takes the presents from the tray and puts them on the table.*)

(*He looks at the clock on the mantelpiece.*) And *now!* Six o'clock. Six o'clock. Where's everybody?

(Olivia *enters from the hall as he is speaking. She has some parcels in her hands.* George *and* Ann *move down* R., *chatting.*)

That's better. *That's* better. Now, who are we short?. (*He looks round.*) Tony! Where's Tony?

Olivia. He's coming. (*She moves behind the table in front of the settee.*)

Ned (*looking again at the clock*). So's Christmas. No, by Jove. (*He laughs.*) It's come! *What* a Christmas.

(Tony *enters from the hall.*)

Ah, Tony! So now we're here, and only just on time. Right. Let's begin. Now, no cheating. One—two—three—go!

Olivia. Come and open my presents, George!

(*Everyone moves to the table.* George *to the* R. *of* Olivia *and* Ann *to the* R. *of* George. *To the* L. *of* Olivia *stand* Mary *and* Enid. Tony *moves to the* R. *of* Ann *and* Ned *to the* L. *of* Enid. *They all begin to open the parcels. There is general noise and chatter.*)

Mary. Perfume! And my favourite Schiaparelli. Oh, Ned, how lovely.

Ned. Smells like crushed cockroaches to me! Glad you like it.

Olivia. Uncle Ned! Silk stockings! Did you buy these for me, yourself?

Ned. I did! *And* tried them on. (*He opens his parcel and discloses a smoking cap.*) And this—*this* for me.

Enid (*holding up a necklace*). Oh, Ned!

Ned. Oh, that's nothing.

Olivia (*moving to the* R. *of* Tony). How sweet of you. (*She holds up two unfolded georgette handkerchiefs—one red and the other blue.*)

(*Everybody looks up at the handkerchiefs.*)

Ann. Tony, darling, how nice. (*She is looking at two unfolded georgette handkerchiefs—one red and one blue.*)

Enid. Oh, Tony, you shouldn't have. (*She is looking at two unfolded georgette handkerchiefs—one red and one blue.*)

Mary. How thoughtful of you, Tony. (*She is looking at two unfolded georgette handkerchiefs—one red and one blue.*)

George. Original chap, you are, Tony.

Ann. It's the thought that counts.

Tony. Well, there can't be any jealousy, anyhow.

Ned. Dammit!—and Dammit! What's this? What! Look here—look, all of you.

(*They all look at* Ned.)

Look what I've got now.

Olivia. What is it, Uncle Ned?

Ned. *That's* what it is. (*He holds up a pair of panties, which he displays proudly across his chest.*)

Olivia (*with a scream, dashing to* Ned *and retrieving them*). That's the pair you were giving *me*, Mother.

(*The telephone rings.* Mary *moves to the writing table and lifts the receiver.*)

Mary. Yes. This is Barrington four-five-seven-o. (*To the others.*) Just a moment, will you? Mr Wares, from the Children's Home. Yes, Mr Wares . . . (*She listens and looks round at the clock.*) Yes. Yes, of course, I'm sure we could. Immediately? . . . Yes. Good-bye. (*She puts down the receiver and turns to the others.*) They want to know if we could come for the Christmas tree as soon as possible. There are one or two of the kids they don't want to keep up too late.

Ned. Certainly we can. Let's go at once. Come along, everybody. We can finish these off later. (*He moves to the archway.*)

(Mary *moves up* R. *by the table.* Enid *follows* Ned.)

Olivia (*moving to the archway*). We can cut across the garden. I'll tell Aunt Topsey.

(Olivia *exits through the hall.*)

Ned. Where's my costume?

Mary. It's in the hall.

Ned. Come along, Enid, my dear. Come along.

(NED *and* ENID *exit through the hall.*)

MARY. Coming, George?
GEORGE. I'd like to, Mrs Meldon. (*He moves to the archway.*)

(MARY *and* GEORGE *exit through the hall.* TONY *and* ANN *are left, looking at each other.* TONY *is about to speak when* OLIVIA, GEORGE, NED *and* MARY *return putting on outdoor clothes and chatting. They move to the french windows, open them and exit.* TOPSEY *enters through the hall, stares at* TONY *and follows the others.*)

TONY. Well—oh, hell! (*He moves to the archway.*)

(NICHOLAS *enters through the hall and collides with* TONY. *Rather amused* ANN *moves below the chair.*)

NICHOLAS. What! Not going to the party, sir?
TONY. Parties—hell!
NICHOLAS. T'ch! T'ch! Not going to a party *there*, I hope!

(TONY *makes a move to depart.*)

Just a moment, sir. If I might . . .
TONY (*rather gruffly*). What is it?
NICHOLAS. Would you do a little sketch of me, sir? I saw the one you did of Mr Ned, and did I laugh! Look at me, sir, I'm the answer to a cartoonist's prayer, aren't I?
ANN. Go on, Tony.
NICHOLAS. Have a shot, sir.
TONY (*laughing*) O.K. (*He takes a small sketchbook and pencil from his pocket and looks at* NICHOLAS. *He moves past* NICHOLAS *to the* R *of the armchair above the fireplace.*)
NICHOLAS. Thank you, sir.
TONY. Hop into that chair. That's the idea.

(NICHOLAS *sits in the chair and* TONY *begins to sketch rapidly.*)

TONY. What are you going to do when you leave here, Mr Nicholas?

(ANN *moves to the* R. *of the settee.*)

NICHOLAS. I've a big job on, sir. Got to be best man at a wedding on Friday. Lovely thing, a wedding, sir.
TONY. There's something in being a bachelor.
NICHOLAS (*with great scorn*). A bachelor! Now I ask you, sir— what *is* a bachelor? Just a traffic light, with the amber, green and red all on at the same time.
TONY (*laughing*). Well, I . . .
NICHOLAS. Oh, no, sir. I wouldn't be a bachelor if I was you.
ANN. I believe you *are* a married man, Mr Nicholas. Have you any children?
NICHOLAS. Swarms of 'em! I've been busy!

Tony (*rising*). Well, here you are—only an outline! (*He holds out the sketch to* Nicholas.)

Nicholas (*rising* L. *of* Tony *and looking at the sketch*). Well! If that don't beat the band! And making me into Father Christmas, too. Whatever made you think of that?

Ann (*running above the settee and standing between them*). Let me see, Tony. Oh, To-ny. It's marvellous.

Tony. Glad you like it. (*He detaches the drawing from the book and hands it to* Nicholas.)

Nicholas. Lovely! I never knew I was so handsome!

Tony. Well, (*he moves to the archway*) I suppose I'd better go to this damn party. Coming, Ann?

Ann. In a few minutes, Tony.

Tony. See you both later.

(Tony *exits through the hall to collect his coat*.)

Nicholas (*as* Tony *disappears; moving to the archway*). And thanks again, sir. (*He moves between the chair and the settee.*) And now, miss, it's time for Cinderella to say *Au Revoir* to her old Father Christmas.

Ann (*moving to the front of the settee*). But—you're not *really* going?

Nicholas. I've got to go, miss. But we'll be meeting again. And, anyway, "Parting is such sweet sorrow," as the discharged convict said to the Governor of the prison.

Ann. But, you can't go away like this—without even . . .

Nicholas (*moving close to the* R. *end of the settee*). I'm not going away "without even"—I've had a wonderful present.

Ann. What is it?

Nicholas. A Christmas costume. Mr Ned gave it to me.

Ann (*sitting at the* L. *end of the settee*). But you must look just—just sweet.

Nicholas. Like to see me in it?

Ann. Yes—rather.

Nicholas. Well (*seriously*) maybe, you will—if you keep your eyes open—especially when no-one else is looking.

Ann. What do you mean?

Nicholas. Never ask a burglar what he means.

Ann. You aren't a burglar.

Nicholas. Aren't I? (*He produces a cigarette-case from his pocket.*) Just look at this.

Ann (*taking it*). Why, it's Tony's. You don't mean to say you—you *stole* it from him? But, why?

Nicholas (*moving to the fireplace*). You see, miss, I was thinking things out all the time he was cartooning—that young man's trembling on the brink of a precipice.

Ann. Precipice?

Nicholas. He only wants a good shove, and he'll propose to you.

Ann. O-oh!

Nicholas. At this moment Mr Tony's saying: "Dammit! I don't want to go to the kids' show. I want to go and talk to *her*. But I've said I'm going to the party, and I can't step down." (*He now speaks very slowly.*) But, if Mr Tony couldn't find his cigarette-case—why, what could be easier for him than to come back here and say . . . "Er . . . Ann, have you seen my cigarette-case?" (*He is mimicking* Tony's *voice and as he does so he makes a commanding gesture towards the archway.*)

(Tony *enters through the hall, he has a sheet of paper in his hand.*)

Tony (*in the archway; hesitatingly*) Ann, have you see my cigarette-case?

(Nicholas, *with a grin of satisfaction, looks at* Ann *and then almost tiptoes out through the hall.*)

Ann (*with a slight giggle*). Yes. I saw it a minute ago. (*She quickly puts the cigarette-case on the settee.*)

Tony (*moving to the* R. *of the settee*).Where?

Ann. Why—(*she points to the settee*) why, it's here.

Tony. How did it get here?

Nicholas (*putting his head in from the corner of the hall entrance*). Magic.

(Ann *laughs;* Nicholas' *head disappears.* Tony *picks up the case, takes a cigarette from it, and offers the case to* Ann.)

Ann (*taking a cigarette*). Thanks.

(Tony *takes a lighter from his pocket, lights both their cigarettes and sits beside* Ann.)

Tony. Why aren't you with the others?

Ann. Why—why aren't *you*, Tony?

Tony. It's a free country.

Ann. I suppose it is. Though one only seems free to do the things one wants to do with the people one *doesn't want*.

Tony. I beg your pardon.

Ann. Oh, nothing—nothing—you'd better hurry along, Tony. They'll only be a few minutes at the Home.

Tony. Yes, I'd better. (*But he makes no attempt to do so.*)

Ann. You—you aren't very happy, are you?

Tony (*bitterly*). Happy? Who's happy? One isn't supposed to be *happy*.

Ann. I'm aw-fully sorry for you, Tony.

Tony. That's nice of you. What are you sorry about? You think I'm sore about Olivia and George?

Ann. Well—you and she seemed to be get-ting along so well.

Tony. Did we? Well, we weren't.

Ann (*with satisfaction*) I'm so glad,

TONY. Don't think me rude about your sister. But she's the most awful bore I ever met. Can't talk about anything but clothes, clothes, clothes. (*Imitating* OLIVIA's *rather dramatic form of speech.*) "Hats are going to be worn rather long this season—and bosoms are going out again."

ANN (*laughing*). Oh, Tony.

TONY. And if you ask her opinion about a drawing, she just squeaks.

ANN. Perhaps that's just because she doesn't understand your work. It isn't always easy for someone who isn't an—an artist to understand.

TONY. Maybe it isn't. Well (*he looks at the drawing in his hand*) surely *that's* obvious enough? (*He thrusts the drawing into* ANN's *hand.*)

(ANN *takes it with a look of horror, then her face brightens.*)

ANN. But this is marvellous. It's Aunt Topsey to the life. It's —it's marvellous.

TONY. Glad you like it.

ANN. You see—that's *you*, Tony. You get the *idea* of everyone in a few lines. That's why your caricatures are so brilliant.

TONY. And that's why I'm going to stick to cartoons. I may not be a Rembrandt, but I might be a Tom Webster. Ann—what a fool I've been. It's *you* who've got the artist's eyes. Not Olivia. It's been you all the time.

ANN. Yes, Tony?

TONY. You're the only girl in the world I care about—that I ever cared about. Ann—do you think you care, too?

ANN. I think . . . (*She hesitates*).

TONY. Yes . . . ?

ANN. If I tried very hard . . .

TONY. Yes . . . ?

ANN. I might learn to care . . .

TONY. Ann!

ANN. A lit-tle.

TONY. Ann—darling. (*He takes her in his arms*)

ANN. Oh, To-ny!

(*He kisses her.*)

Oh, To-ny.

TONY. You're not offended?

ANN (*putting up her lips for him*). I'm furious. (*She giggles.*) Do it again.

(TONY *kisses her again.* NED, *followed by* TOPSEY *and* ENID, *enter from the hall.* NED *is wearing his smoking cap.*)

NED (*moving between the chair and the settee; triumphantly*). Well, *that* didn't take long. (*He glances at* ANN *and* TONY.) Apparently it didn't take long enough.

(ANN *and* TONY *break, and rise.*)

And wasn't I a success?
ENID (*holding his* L. *arm*). I should think you were.

(TOPSEY *moves above the settee.*)

NED. But the life and soul of the party was—who do you think
it was? Eh, Ann, who do you think?
ANN. Who?
NED. Aunt Topsey!
TOPSEY. Rubbish, Ned. (*She moves to the armchair above the fire-place and sits.*) I never said a word!
NED. That's what I mean. (*He laughs.*) And *now*, I think, we
deserve a little drink. (*He moves to the table up* R.) Come on, Tony,
give a hand.

(TONY *moves to* NED, *and helps with the drinks.* ENID *sits on the* R.
arm of the settee. NED *pours out a drink and takes it to* TOPSEY, *then
returns to the table up* R.)

TONY. What will it be, Mother?

(TONY *holds up a bottle and* ENID *nods in agreement.*)

The usual, Ann?
ANN. Please.

(MARY *enters from the hall.*)

NED (*turning as* MARY *enters*). I'm playing fast and loose with
the jug and bottle department, Mary.

(TONY *moves to* ENID *and* ANN *and offers them a drink.*)

MARY (*moving to the* R. *of* TOPSEY). That's right, Ned.
NED (*to* TOPSEY, *raising the decanter*). Tipsey—Topsey.
TONY (*to* MARY). *Tiny* whisky? (*He moves to the table up* R.)
MARY. The noun's right, Tony, but you could improve on the
adjective.
TONY (*laughing*). Splendid! (*He pours out the drinks.*)
NED (*looking around*). Where's Olivia—and George?
MARY (*moving to the fireplace*). Olivia was talking to him as we
came out.

(TONY *moves to* MARY *and* TOPSEY *with the drinks.*)

ANN. I expect she's found a nice little job for George.
NED (*moving below the chair*). Well, I can't wait. I must tell you
all something. I must give you all a great surprise. I want to
introduce (*with a flourish*) the future Mrs Ned Meldon.
ANN (*kneeling on the settee and kissing* ENID). Gracious, Uncle Ned
What a surprise!
TONY (*moving between* NED *and* ENID). So you and mother have
really . . . ? Gosh! (*He moves down* R.)

Ned (*proudly*). We have.

Ann. Congratulations, Enid.

Ned. It's I that need the congratulations. (*To* Enid.) Took long enough over it, didn't I?

Enid. Only eleven years, Ned.

Ned. Now, Topsey, what are you going to say to her?

(Topsey *looks at* Enid, *searches for the right phrase, and shouts it out with customary vigour.*)

Topsy (*to* Enid). Many happy returns.

Ned. Now—now—now.

Topsey (*with unexpected graciousness*). I hope you'll both be very happy, my dears.

Ned. That's grand of you, Topsey. (*He looks at* Enid, *then to* Mary.) Dammit, Mary. Doesn't she look lovely?

Mary (*moving to* Enid *and kissing her*). She certainly does. (*She sits on the settee.*)

Enid. And I haven't any lipstick on.

Ned. In that case . . . (*He kisses* Enid *heartily.*)

Enid. Oh, Ned!

Mary (*lifting her glass*). To the happy pair!

(Olivia *and* George *enter from the hall.*)

All. To the happy pair.

George. Gee, Olivia. (*He looks entirely bewildered.*) How *did* they guess? Thanks a lot, folks.

(George *and* Olivia *move down stage a few paces.*)

Tony. What! Really?

George. Go on. Tell them, Olivia.

Olivia. Well—George and I . . .

Ned. So that's the way of it? (*He moves above the writing table.*) Well, I'll give you another toast—To the second happy pair.

Mary. Well—I . . .

Enid. Congratulations!

(Olivia *moves to the* r. *of* Enid *and* George *moves to the* r. *of* Topsey. Alice *enters from the hall.*)

Ann. Stout work, Olivia. Congrats.

Tony (*speaking with meaning in his voice*). Come over here, Ann. I want to ask you a question.

(Ann *rises and moves to* Tony. Ned *hands a glass of sherry—already poured out—to* Alice. Alice *drinks.*)

Ned (*moving to the radiogram*). And now, what about a little music? (*He bends over the cabinet.*) What's on?

(Enid *rises moves to the table* r, *and pours out two drinks.*)

Olivia (*glancing at her watch and moving to the armchair down* L.). Carols, I think!

Ned. What could be better? (*He bends down, switches on the lights on the Christmas tree and switches on the wireless.*) Dammit!

(Olivia *sits in the armchair.*)

Mary. What is it, Uncle Ned?

Ned. No-one's got a drink for the poor old gentleman.

Enid (*moving to* Ned, *with two glasses and handing him one*). Oh, yes, they have. Your wife has.

(*The wireless gradually comes on. Carol singers can be heard singing "Good King Wenceslas".*)

Ned (*taking the glass*). Bless you, my dear. Now, come on, gather round.

During the last few moments of this scene the grouping is arranging itself around the fire. The armchair R. *of the fireplace is used by* Topsey, *whilst the others are sitting on the ground around and in front of the fire.* Mary, Enid *and* Ned *form a group by the window; they stand close together with their glasses raised.* Alice *moves* L.C., *lifting her glass to* Mary *in the group by the window. The lights fade gradually through this and the carol music begins. The music mounts in volume as the lights fade to* Black-Out *and when this is complete the transparency slowly lights up revealing* Mr Nicholas.

The entire cast now joins vigorously in singing the chosen carol. Nicholas *slowly raises his hand upwards in the form of a benediction. The transparency lights slowly fade as—*

the Curtain *falls*

FURNITURE AND PROPERTY PLOT

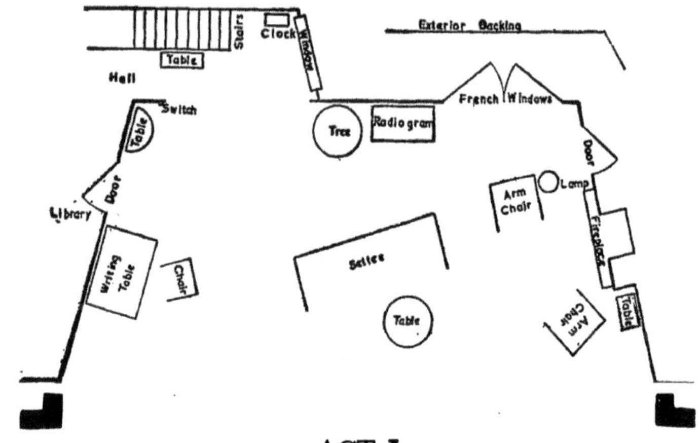

ACT I

On stage:

Settee. *On it:* cushions.

Writing table. *On it:* telephone, writing materials, Christmas cards, labels, box of cigarettes, box of matches, ashtray, vase of holly.

Chair.

2 armchairs. *On them:* cushions, magazines.

Radiogram. *On it:* ukelele, box of chocolates, magazine.

Table. *On it:* papers, cartoon, ashtray.

Table. *On it:* drinks, decanter, glasses.

Coffee table. *On it:* ashtray, playing cards, box of matches.

Table in the hall. *On it:* vase of holly.

Standard lamp.

Clock in the hall.

Christmas tree decorated and wired with coloured lights.

Mirror.

On the mantelpiece: Christmas cards, clock, cigarette box, box of matches, ashtray.

On the walls: one or two pictures, holly and balloons.

Poker in fireplace.

Off R.:

Cloak (OLIVIA).

Personal:

TOPSEY: garment, knitting-needles, bag. *In it:* card.

TONY: letters, cigarette-case, woollen garments.

NED: tobacco pouch, pipe, box of matches.

ACT II

Set:
Topsey's knitting on radiogram.

Off R.:
Tray with pot of tea, cups and saucers, sandwiches, cakes (Alice).

Personal:
Alice: duster.
Ned: paper money, lipstick, watch, pouch with a playing card concealed inside, pipe, box of matches.
Ann: lipstick, Father Christmas costume, handkerchief.
Nicholas: pipe.
Enid: handbag with compact and lipstick.

ACT III

Off L.:
Father Christmas costume (Nicholas).

Personal:
Ann: handbag. *In it:* lighter.
Mary: parcels.
Tony: parcels, sketch-book and pencil, sketch, lighter.
Topsey: knitting, wool, handbag with envelopes, ring.
Ned: beard, smoking cap.
George: tray with parcels.
Olivia: parcels, watch.
Nicholas: cigarette-case with cigarettes.

AUTHOR'S NOTE

The Carol Records. Carol records of children's voices without those of adults if possible—are not easy to come by.

In the author's production some of the records were made by a group of boys from a local school and recorded locally on wax—an inexpensive procedure. Recording on tape would also be effective. The carol *Good King Wenceslas* was used throughout the play as required. *Silent Night* was used on page 46; and if the record is a good one, it pays to play it through the entire two verses whilst the old men sit by the fire, holding their positions motionless perhaps for the first verse, but changing them during the second with, maybe, Nicholas gently beating time with is pipe.

The Transparency. The transparency behind which Mr Nicholas takes his place, is best situated in approximately the position of the picture on the stairs. It can occupy a similar situation whether the stairs are actually shown or not, and whether there is an archway in use or not.

The transparency merely replaces the canvas in a portion of the flat in question. It is a piece of gauze painted in exactly the same manner as the rest of the flats in the room. Behind this piece of gauze, another one painted in the same way—or rather darker for preference—is attached by drawing pins to the top of the flat to form an additional light shield during the action of the play.

At the moment of the stage black-out being complete, in the final scene of the play, Nicholas, standing behind the gauze, unpins and lets drop the second piece of material. The gauze lights —preferably two 100 watt, one red and one orange, on either side behind the gauze—are then slowly brought up on dimmers to full strength, held for a little and then dimmed again.

The whole process is completely simple to construct and work, causes no extra trouble and is highly effective.

The Snow. A little trouble will repay handsomely. The snow should be liberal in quantity, and the change of climatic conditions at the end of Act I should be clearly and unmistakably seen by the entire audience. There is no necessity for them to be acutely aware of the nature of the backing behind the windows in the early part of this act. But a small flat painted to represent a snow-clad country scene, and inserted behind the window during that period in the first act in which the curtains are closed, or the introduction of the snow-covered branch of a conifer, is a necessity—one which is simplicity itself to improvise.